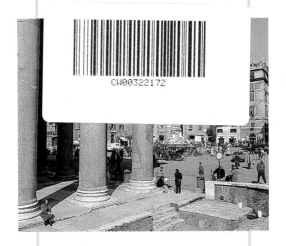

Rome

by Jane Shaw

Jane Shaw grew up in Edinburgh and lived in London for several years before fleeing to Rome in the early 1990s, where she lives in the heart of Trastevere, writing, editing and translating. She has contributed to guide books to Rome and Italy for Time Out, Dorling Kindersley and Insight, among others.

Above: *The Pantheon, Piazza Rotonda*

AA Publishing

Above: *A Swiss Guard at the Vatican*

Written by Jane Shaw

First published in 1998
Reprinted Jun and Nov 1998; Jun 1999
Reprinted 2001. Information verified and updated
Reprinted Feb and Aug 2002
Reprinted 2004. Information verified and updated
Reprinted March 2004. Reprinted May, Aug and Dec 2004
Reprinted Feb 2005.
Reprinted 2006. Information updated and verified.
Reprinted Aug 2006
Reprinted Feb 2007

© Automobile Association Developments Limited 2004, 2006

Published by AA Publishing, a trading name of Automobile Association Developments Limited, whose registered office is Fanum House, Basing View, Basingstoke, Hampshire RG21 4EA.
Registered number 1878835.

A03309

Colour separation: Keenes, Andover
Printed and bound in Italy by Printer Trento S.r.l.

Find out more about AA Publishing and the wide range of travel publications and services the AA provides by visiting our website at www.theAA.com/travel

Contents

About this Book 4

Viewing Rome 5–14
Jane Shaw's Rome	6
Rome's Features	7
Essence of Rome	8–9
The Shaping of Rome	10–11
Peace and Quiet	12–13
Rome's Famous	14

Top Ten 15–26
Campidoglio	16
Castel Sant'Angelo	17
Colosseum (Colosseo)	18
Palazzo Barberini	19
Pantheon	20
Piazza Navona	21
Roman Forum (Foro Romano)	22
San Clemente	23
Sistine Chapel & Vatican Museums	24–25
St. Peter's (San Pietro)	26

What to See 27–90
Rome	30–79
In the Know	34–35
Food and Drink	50–51
Excursions from the City	80–90

Where To 91–116
Eat and Drink	92–9
Stay	100–103
Shop	104–109
Take the Children	110–111
Be Entertained	112–116

Practical Matters 117–124

Index 125–6

Acknowledgements 126

About this Book

KEY TO SYMBOLS

✚ map reference to the maps found in the What to See section (see below)

✉ address or location

☎ telephone number

🕐 opening times

🍴 restaurant or café on premises or nearby

Ⓜ nearest underground train station

🚌 nearest bus/tram route

🚆 nearest overground train station

🚢 ferry crossings and excursions by boat

✈ travel by air

ℹ tourist information

♿ facilities for visitors with disabilities

✋ admission charge

↔ other places of interest nearby

❓ other practical information

➤ indicates the page where you will find a fuller description

---

This book divided into five sections to cover the most important aspects of your visit to Rome.

Viewing Rome pages 5–14
An introduction to Rome by the author.
  Rome's Features
  Essence of Rome
  The Shaping of Rome
  Peace and Quiet
  Rome's Famous

Top Ten pages 15–26
The author's choice of the Top Ten places to visit in Rome, each with practical information.

What to See pages 27–90
The two main areas of Rome, each with its own brief introduction and an alphabetical listing of the main attractions.
  Practical information
  Snippets of 'Did You Know...' information
  4 suggested walks
  2 suggested tours
  2 features

Where To... pages 91–116
Detailed listings of the best places to eat, stay, shop, take the children and be entertained.

Practical Matters pages 117–24
A highly visual section containing essential travel information.

Maps
All map references are to the individual maps found in the What to See section of this guide.
For example, Galleria Borghese has the reference ✚ 29D4—indicating the page on which the map is located and the grid square in which the gallery is to be found.
A list of the maps that have been used in this travel guide can be found in the index.

Prices
Where appropriate, an indication of the cost of an establishment is given by € signs:
€€€ denotes higher prices, €€ denotes average prices, while € denotes lower charges.

Star Ratings
Most of the places described in this book have been given a separate rating:
✪✪✪   Do not miss
✪✪   Highly recommended
✪   Worth seeing

Viewing
Rome

Jane Shaw's Rome 6
Rome's Features 7
Essence of Rome 8–9
The Shaping of
    Rome 10–11
Peace and Quiet 12–13
Rome's Famous 14

Above: *Castel Sant'Angelo*
Right: *Shopping by scooter*

5

Jane Shaw's Rome

Vatican City
Rome is the capital of the Roman Catholic church, for in it lies the Vatican City (Città del Vaticano), covering less than half a hectare, and really a separate state with its own post office, radio and TV stations. Rome abounds in nuns, monks and priests from all over the world who come to study at one of the Catholic universities; in and around St. Peter's you can see an exotic array of the habits worn by various religious orders.

St. Peter's is impressive even at dusk

Rome has got it all—a climate that gives sunny days at any time of year, a cuisine that has something (and usually a lot of things) for all tastes and some of the best fine art and architecture in the world. This is a city of contrasts; a bustling, modern capital set amid ancient splendour where screeching *motorini* swoop past leisurely pedestrians, classical art competes for attention with high fashion, and a beautiful sunny day can suddenly throw up a sky-blackening storm with thunder like cannon fire and rain that'll soak you in seconds.

It helps to approach it with a flexible attitude. You may not always be able to achieve what you set out to do (museums, shops, restaurants and even occasionally banks sometimes close suddenly for one reason or another), but don't worry. There are plenty of other things to do and even the streetlife, with its constantly changing parade of locals and visitors alike, is worth watching from a pavement or piazza bar. There are intriguing juxtapositions everywhere: In narrow winding streets of terracotta buildings clothes boutiques nestle among family-run grocers, craft studios, art galleries and restaurants.

The weather helps create a relaxed way of life in which even the most simple transaction may need far more time than you would have thought possible. On the other hand, lunch can take all afternoon so you'll probably soon stop worrying that the overseas post takes rather longer than expected. There is notorious bureaucracy and time-consuming public service (but these are improving), but once you adjust to the pace of life, you realise how much of Rome functions extremely efficiently, including the bus service, which gets you where you want in central Rome more or less when you want.

The beauty of Rome is a magnet to artists, tourists and students, many of whom never quite manage to leave it.

Rome's Features

Population

The city of Rome is roughly 2,700 years old. It has a population of about 2.5 million—up from 200,000 in 1870 when Italy became a unified nation (although there were well over 1 million people living in the city in the days of the empire). There are about 200,000 foreigners resident in Rome. About 10 million people arrive at Fiumicino airport every year. Over half of the working population are in government administration; few work in industry—over 100,000, while around 600,000 people work in offices. The city covers about 585sq miles (1,500sq km) and 12 hills, having expanded from the original seven hills of Rome.

Climate

The best seasons for visiting are April to June, September and October—also the busiest, although the real peak comes at Easter when pilgrims swell the crowds of tourists. The average annual temperature is 16°C (61°F) with a high of 38°C (100°F) and a low of -4°C (25°F).

Crime

The bag-snatching and pocket-picking sectors of the Roman criminal community pose the biggest threat to visitors. Here there is good news and bad. Bag-snatches, called *scippi* and traditionally committed by masked figures on motor scooters have been on the decrease, but the number of picked pockets has been on the rise; take care on the 64 bus to St. Peter's and around the Termini train station.

In July and August temperatures can reach 40°C (104°F) and in August a lot of businesses close for the holidays. Early spring and late autumn are the wettest seasons (you can be unlucky at other times as well)—Rome has a similar annual rainfall to London but most falls over a few days. Even in winter the weather can be glorious with maximum daily temperatures around 15°C (59°F) but, although it seldom snows, there can be bitingly cold winds in December, January and early February.

Carabinieri police watch the world go by in Piazza Venezia

Churches and Bars

Central Rome has over 400 churches, about 600 bars and less than 40 toilets (but most bars will allow you to use theirs). There are also 150km (93 miles) of holes in the road.

Essence of Rome

Central Rome on both sides of the Tiber (Tevere) is a city of contrasts. This busy modern capital is squeezed into a maze of old streets in which the layers of more than 2,000 years of history are superimposed on each other: ancient columns

Legend has it that Romulus and Remus were breast-fed by a wolf and founded Rome; the beautiful and busy Piazza Navona

embedded in Renaissance palaces, baroque façades slapped on to the front of Romanesque churches and 1930s fascist office buildings nestling among it all. Not only is Rome the seat of the Italian government (both the President and the Prime Minister have their official residences here), but it is also a world centre for the film and fashion industries.

THE **10** ESSENTIALS

*If you only have a short time to visit Rome,
or would like to get a really complete picture of the
city, here are the essentials:*

• **Go to the Vatican** and
marvel at Michelangelo's
masterpieces in the Sistine
Chapel (➤ 24).

• **Look down on Rome
from on high** (➤ 34 for
suggested view points), and
try to find the flattish dome

• **Walk the streets at the
Forum** where Julius Caesar
trod (➤ 22).

• **At St. Peter's look on the
floor of the central aisle**
(➤ 26) where the lengths of
other cathedrals' aisles are
marked—see how your local
one measures up.

• **Do the historic centre
walk** (➤ 26) to take you
past some of the most
famous tourist sights in the
world.

• **Try to imagine the
Colosseum** (➤ 18) full of
raucous crowds with wild
animals and hapless humans
fighting it out in the ring.

• **Throw a coin into the
Trevi Fountain** (➤ 40)
which guarantees your
return. Italian currency ends
up in the coffers of the town
council; foreign coins are
donated to the Red Cross.

with a hole in
the middle,
which is the
Pantheon
(➤ 20).

• **Find a bar
on Piazza
Navona**
(➤ 21) or
Campo de'
Fiori (➤ 37),
sip a drink and
watch life
saunter by.

• **See Rome by night,**
preferably on foot. Many of
the main monuments are
floodlit and those that are
not have an eerie beauty in
the city's soft street lighting.

• **Visit the church of Santa
Maria in Cosmedin** (➤ 68)
to test your nerve with your
hand in the *Bocca della
Verità* (mouth of truth), which
will bite if you tell a lie.

*Illuminated Santa Maria in
Trastevere creates an
atmospheric meeting
place; Piazza Navona's
cafés are popular by day*

The Shaping of Rome

753BC
Rome founded by Romulus, the first of seven kings.

616–576BC
Under Tarquin the Elder the Forum and Circo Massimo are established.

509BC
Tarquin the Proud, last of the kings, expelled and Brutus establishes the Republic.

312BC
Via Appia Antica started and Aqua Appia, the first aqueduct.

168BC
Rome conquers Greece.

149–146BC
Carthage destroyed in third Punic war.

60BC
Julius Caesar, Crassus and Pompey form the Triumvirate.

51BC
Conquest of Gaul.

44BC
Murder of Julius Caesar.

27BC
Augustus becomes the first emperor.

AD64
Fire destroys much of the city (Emperor Nero plays his fiddle).

AD67
Crucifixion of St. Peter and execution of St. Paul during first persecution of Christians.

312
Battle of Milvian bridge, Constantine wins control of the Empire.

380
Christianity becomes the Roman Empire's official religion.

395
Empire divided into two parts, Eastern and Western.

410
Rome sacked by Goths.

455
Rome sacked by Vandals.

475
Fall of Western Roman Empire.

778
Charlemagne conquers Italy.

961
King Otto of the Saxons becomes first Holy Roman Emperor.

1300
First Holy Year proclaimed by Pope Boniface VIII.

1309
Pope Clement V moves papacy to Avignon

1347
Cola di Rienzo tries to establish a new Roman Republic.

1377
Papacy returns from Avignon.

1378
Great Schism in papacy, a second 'pope' is established in Avignon.

1409
A third papacy established in Pisa.

1417
Pope Martin V ends the Great Schism.

1453
Fall of Constantinople to the Turks, marking end of Eastern Empire.

1498–1502
Papacy at war with Italian states.

1508–1512
Papacy at war with Romagna.

1520
Martin Luther's reforming thesis starts the Reformation.

1527
Rome sacked by Charles V and German and Spanish troops.

1545–63
Council of Trent leads to the Counter Reformation

An impression of the Tiber in ancient times

to strengthen the Catholic church against reforming Protestants.

1585
Pope Sixtus V plans new city with many new streets and buildings.

1600
Giordano Bruno burned at stake in Campo de' Fiori.

1626
New St. Peter's consecrated.

1797
Napoleon captures Rome.

1801
Concordat between Pope Pius VII and Napoleon.

1806
Holy Roman Empire ends.

1808
Rome occupied by French; Pius VII sent to France in captivity.

1814
Pius VII returns to Rome.

1820
Wars for Italian Unification begin.

1849–66
French troops in Rome protect the Pope from the armies of Unification.

1861
Kingdom of Italy formed under King Vittorio Emanuele.

1870
Rome captured by General Garibaldi's troops; Italian Unification complete.

1922
Mussolini marches on Rome, becomes Prime Minister.

1929
Lateran Treaty between Mussolini and the papacy creates Vatican state.

1940
Italy enters World War II.

1943
Mussolini resigns and Germans take over.

1944
Allies liberate Rome from Germans.

1946
Republic established, King Umberto II exiled.

1957
Treaty of Rome establishes Common Market (now European Union).

1960
Olympic games held in Rome.

1978
Prime Minister Aldo Moro assassinated.

1981
Pope John Paul II shot in St. Peter's square.

1993
Anti-corruption movement starts in Italy; two bombs explode—at San Giovanni in Laterano and at San Giorgio in Velabro. Mafia blamed.

2000
Many millions of pilgrims descend on Rome for the Holy Year.

2005
Pope John Paul II dies and Pope Benedict XV1 is elected as his successor.

Peace & Quiet

One of the ancient bridges linking Isola Tiberina to the river bank

Wild Cats
Although not exactly wild, Rome is famous for its cats, many of whom live in the streets or among the ruins relying on the goodwill of local people, or informal cat protection organizations, to feed them. The recent increase in these charitable souls may have something to do with the increasing boldness of some of the local rats (although don't worry, you are no more likely to come across a rat than you are in any other major city).

Rome is not a quiet city. Heavy traffic and vast numbers of tourists combine to make sightseeing a tiring, sometimes stressful, business, particularly in the spring, early summer and autumn. But do not despair, even in the packed historic core it is possible to come across havens of peace—a little piazza or quiet alley—where you can sit for a moment or two. Some of the sights themselves are often relatively tranquil. The Palatino, Piazza Farnese, the Terme di Caracalla and Circo Massimo, for example, are usually fairly empty, and on the hill above Circo Massimo the town's rose garden will refresh your senses and restore your energy levels.

Parks and Gardens
There are a number of parks and gardens in or near the heart of the city. The most central of these is Villa Borghese which stretches out behind the Pincio Gardens above Piazza del Popolo (➤ 59). Here there are lakes, flower gardens, trees and rolling hillsides on which to rest. Above the Colosseum is the Colle Oppio, a slightly run-down turn-of-the-century style park that contains the ruins of Nero's Golden House and Trajan's baths as well as some inviting benches. On the other side of the Colosseum is the park of Villa Celimontana (entrance on Piazza della Navicella) laid out as formal gardens for the Mattei family in the 16th century. Off Via di Santa Sabina on the Aventine hill there's the Parco di San Alessio and a most delightful orangery with good views over Trastevere. In Trastevere itself you will find the botanical gardens (on Via Corsini off Via della Lungara), pretty Villa Sciarra (entrance on Via Calandrelli) built on a steep hillside and the massive Villa Doria Pamphili (entrance on Via di San Pancrazio) with its statues, trees, fountains and artificial river.

Roman Wildlife
The crumbling masonry of ancient Rome contains a wide array of plants, small animals and birds. In the 19th century, for example,

several specific studies of the flora of the Colosseum were made and hundreds of plant species were identified. Many of these have since disappeared but in spring there is still a flamboyant display of wild and semi-wild flowers sprouting up in the Fori Imperiali (► 40). If you look carefully, you may catch sight of little birds or scuttling lizards, particularly the green-grey Sicilian lizard or even the far rarer green lizard. Geckos, on the other hand, are everywhere. The more exotic birdlife includes the blue rock thrush, the black redstart, little owls and kestrels.

The most famous of the city's trees are the pines of Rome, the aptly named umbrella pine (*Pinus pinea*). Many of the palm trees were planted at the end of the 19th century while orange trees, which sometimes drop their soggy fruit at the feet of passers-by, have long been used to decorate palace and convent gardens.

Finally, a word of warning for hayfever sufferers: the plane trees that line the river and some of the main streets emit a particularly potent pollen in spring.

National Park

Those who want to get right away from the city head off to the Parco Nazionale d'Abruzzo, 156sq miles (400sq km) of alpine scenery which includes some of the highest peaks in the Apennine range (5,560ft/2,000m and above) and a network of well sign-posted walking, rambling and hiking routes. The park boasts a spectacular range of (admittedly rather shy) animals and birds including bears, wolves, chamonix, lynx, wild boars (which also feature on some local menus), eagles, falcons and owls. The middle of the park is Pescasseroli reached by bus from Via Tiburtina or car by way of Licenza or Subiaco.

Peaceful today; Circo Massimo was once the site of chariot races and blood sports

Rome's Famous

St. Peter was martyred here in AD67

As the former capital of the Roman Empire, the headquarters of the Roman Catholic church and the capital of modern Italy, it is hardly surprising that Rome has attracted a vast array of talented and important people from all professions.

One former resident who went on to true greatness, as guardian of the gates of Heaven, was St. Peter. Christ's disciple came to Rome around AD42. He was one of the first Christian martyrs and was crucified (upside down as he felt unworthy of dying as Christ had) in AD67 under Emperor Nero.

Artists

The artists who came to Rome include Michelangelo (1475–1564) who was here from 1506. This tempestuous, troubled genius is believed to have been homosexual and always used male models, even when representing women. In contrast, Raphael (1483–1520) who came to Rome in 1508, fell in love with one of his models—the *Fornarina* (baker's daughter) (► 19). Caravaggio (1571–1610) was in Rome from 1591 until he had to flee justice in 1606 after killing his tennis opponent in a fight.

Monarchs

Among the monarchs who sought refuge was Queen Christina of Sweden (1626–89) who was welcomed by the Pope after her conversion to Catholicism. In 1715 another Catholic royal, James Edward Stuart (1688–1766), fled here after his unsuccessful attempt to win back the British throne for his family. His son, Charles Edward (Bonnie Prince Charlie), was born here in 1721 and died at Palazzo Balestra near Piazza Venezia in 1788.

Napoleon

Napoleon Bonaparte arrived in Rome at the head of his conquering army in 1797. After his defeat and death in 1821 his family continued to live here.

Writers

Visiting writers include Johann Wolfgang Goethe (1749–1832) who lived on Via del Corso from 1786 to 1788. Henry James (1843–1916) was a frequent visitor, while the English 19th-century poets Keats, Shelley, Byron, Robert Browning and Elizabeth Barrett-Browning all knew the city well. Author Alberto Moravia (1907–90) was born in Rome; many of his novels and stories are set here.

Film Directors

Two of the most famous film-makers of the 20th century set some of their best works in Rome and are still fondly remembered by those who knew them. Federico Fellini's (1920–93) *La Dolce Vita* became synonymous with Rome in the 1960s, especially the scene where Marcello Mastroianni follows Anita Ekberg into the Fontana di Trevi. Pier Paolo Pasolini (1922–75) used a mixture of contemporary and historic settings for his erudite films. He was brutally murdered in 1975 on the coast near Rome.

Top Ten

Campidoglio	16
Castel Sant'Angelo	17
Colosseum (Colosseo)	18
Palazzo Barberini	19
Pantheon	20
Piazza Navona	21
Roman Forum (Foro Romano)	22
San Clemente	23
Sistine Chapel & Vatican Museums	24–25
St. Peter's (San Pietro)	26

Above: *The Colosseum*
Right: *Angel, Ponte Sant'Angelo*

1
Campidoglio

www.museicapitolini.org

✚ 28C2

✉ Piazza del Campidoglio 1

☎ 06 6710 2475/06 3996 7800 (recorded information)

🕐 Tue–Sat 9–8

🚌 44, 46, 75, 84, 715, 716, 780, 781, 810, 916 to Piazza Venezia

♿ Access only available if you call in advance

✋ Expensive

Piazza del Campidoglio is home to the art and sculpture collections of the Capitoline Museums

The Capitoline Museums house one of Europe's most impressive collections of ancient sculpture—started by the popes in the 15th century.

Michelangelo designed Rome's magnificent civic centre, although later architects finished the job. Today, only the salmon-pink Palazzo Senatorio is used for political purposes (the mayor's office is here), while the flanking buildings form the Campidoglio (or Capitoline) Museums.

On entering the restored Palazzo Nuovo, on the left, you are greeted by the enormous 2nd-century AD bronze equestrian statue of Emperor Marcus Aurelius which rested atop the pedestal in the centre of the square until 1981. On the first floor in room 1 (Sala 1), is a superbly modelled, sensual *Dying Gaul*; like many sculptures here, this is a Roman copy in marble of an earlier Greek work. Roman heads abound, including portraits of philosophers (a whole roomful) and eminent citizens with elaborate hair. The erotic *Capitoline Venus* has a chamber to herself.

The Palazzo Nuovo links by underground passage—known as Gallery Junction—to the restored Palazzo dei Conservatori. In the Conservatori courtyard are giant hands, a head and feet—fragments from a colossal statue of Constantine found in the Forum. Upstairs, highlights include the creamy marble *Venus Esquilina* and the delightfully realistic 1st century BC bronze *Spinario*, a young boy extracting a thorn from his foot. The *She-Wolf Suckling Romulus and Remus* in the Sala della Lupa will be familiar to many—the symbol of Rome is reproduced everywhere. The wolf is thought to be an Etruscan bronze of the late 6th to early 5th centuries BC to which the twins were added in the 16th century.

Paintings include works by Pietro da Cortona, Guido Reni, Tintoretto, Rubens, Van Dyck, Velázquez, Titan; Caravaggio's sensual *St. John the Baptist* in his fully-fledged realist style and Guercino's immense *Burial of St. Petronilla* stand out.

2
Castel Sant'Angelo

This powerful monument on the Tiber symbolizes almost 2,000 years of Roman history, from Hadrian to Italian Unification.

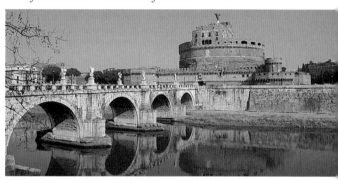

Castel Sant'Angelo was central to the history of the papacy and the defence of the city until 1886 when it was turned into a museum. It is a labyrinth of a place both literally and historically.

Built by Emperor Hadrian (AD117–138) as a mausoleum to himself, visitors today enter via the original Roman passageway, up which the funeral procession passed. This joins up with one of the medieval ramps that were added when the tomb was converted into a defensive fortress. The dark ramp finally opens on to a courtyard (originally the funerary garden), where now there is Montelupo's statue of an angel (1544) sheathing a sword, commemorating (along with the monument's name) a legendary event in which an angel was seen over Rome at the end of a plague in 590.

Off the courtyard (with its Michelangelo façade from 1514) is the *Sala di Apollo* (1548), exquisitely decorated with ornate *grotteschi* (frescoes); illuminated windows in the floor give you a view down to the underground corridors that led to a notorious papal prison. Following Medici Pope Clement VII's seven-month siege inside the *Castello* (1527), the popes felt they needed more sumptuous apartments. Farnese Pope Paul III (1534–49) commissioned the magnificent *Sala Paolina*, with its beautiful frescoes and *trompe l'oeil* doors. Off the library (with gorgeous stucco work) is the wood-lined papal treasury, the room believed to have held Hadrian's tomb, although the whereabouts of his remains are a mystery. The tour finishes with a walk around the ramparts.

+ 28B4

✉ Lungotevere Castello 50

☎ 06 681 9111/06 3996 .7600 (recorded information)

🕐 Tue–Sun 9–8; ticket office closes at 7

🍴 Café (€)

Ⓜ Lepanto

🚌 34, 40, 62, to Piazza Cavour

✋ Moderate

Castel Sant'Angelo has been mausoleum, fortress, papal prison and museum

17

3
Colosseum (Colosseo)

✠ 29D2

✉ Piazza del Colosseo

☎ 06 3996 7700

🕐 9 to 1 hour before sunset; last ticket 1 hour before closing

🚇 Colosseo

🚌 60, 75, 81, 85, 87, 117, 175 to Piazza del Colosseo

♿ Few

✋ Expensive; joint ticket with Palatino

❓ English language tours at 9.30, 10.15, 11.15, 12.30 and 3

The Colosseum takes its name from the Colossus of Nero, a huge bronze statue which once stood close by

Built in the 1st century AD as a gift to the Romans, this dignified, round monument has become the city's most recognizable symbol.

Emperor Vespasian commissioned the Colosseum to fill the site of a massive lake that his predecessor, Nero, had had excavated for his own private use. The massive circus, with a capacity of more than 55,000, was used for popular, bloodthirsty spectator sports. In spite of centuries of use as an unofficial marble quarry for Renaissance and baroque builders, much of the outer shell has survived showing the four arched tiers (each arch held a statue) behind which staircases and galleries led to the auditorium. Seating was segregated according to sex and status; the emperor's box was at the southern end (opposite today's main entrance) and below him sat the Vestal Virgins.

Nearly all the events staged here guaranteed the bloody death of human participants. Gladiators were usually slaves, prisoners of war or condemned prisoners but the enthusiastic following that a successful gladiator provoked encouraged some upper-class men to train for combat. Other spectacles involved mismatched rivals fighting to the death with nets, tridents and other weapons; fights against wild animals were also popular. The labyrinth of underground passages, lifts and cages through which these unfortunate beasts were channelled into the ring can be seen under the arena. Gladiatorial combat was banned in the 5th century, and changing public tastes led to the Colosseum falling out of use by the 6th century.

4
Palazzo Barberini

A treasure trove of paintings from the 13th to the 16th centuries is housed in one of Rome's grandest baroque palaces.

Carlo Maderno's original design, begun in 1624 for Barberini Pope Urban VIII, was embellished by Bernini and Maderno's nephew Borromini. The latter added the elegant oval staircase and the windows of the upper storey which, using ingenious artificial perspective, preserve the symmetry of the façade while staying in proportion with the size of the actual rooms.

The palace was sold to the Italian state in 1949 and houses, together with Palazzo Corsini (➤ 53), the national

The palace itself is as beautiful as the art it houses

collection of art—Galleria Nazionale d'Arte Antica. Extensive renovations are bringing the main rooms back to their original splendour, the most spectacular of which is the *Gran Salone*, with its elaborate ceiling fresco, *Triumph of Divine Providence*, by Pietro da Cortona. Another highlight is the bedroom of Princess Cornelia Costanza Barberini and Prince Giulio Cesare Colonna di Sciarra.

Magnificent *quattrocento* panel paintings include an ethereal *Annunciation* by Filippo Lippi, and a *Madonna and Saints* by Alunno. The highlights of the collection are the 16th- and 17th-century paintings: Andrea del Sarto's magical *Sacra Famiglia*; Raphael's *La Fornarina* (widely believed to be a portrait of the baker's daughter who was his mistress, although some maintain it is in fact a picture of a courtesan and was painted by Giulio Romano); a portrait of Urban VIII by Bernini (his genius lay more in sculpture and architecture); and works by El Greco, Bronzino, Guido Reni, Guercino and Caravaggio.

✠ 29D4

✉ Via Quattro Fontane 13

☎ 06 32810 (for palace guided tours); gallery 06 481 4430

🕐 Tue–Sun 9–7

Ⓜ Barberini

🚌 52, 53, 56, 61, 62, 63, 80, 95, 116, 119 to Via del Tritone

♿ Few

✋ Moderate

TOP TEN

5

Pantheon

> *Its massive circular interior, lit only
> by a round opening in the roof, is one of the most
> awe–inspiring sights of Rome.*

*The incredible dome of
the Pantheon*

✚ 28C3

✉ Piazza della Rotonda

☎ 06 6830 0230

🕐 Mon–Sat 8.30–7.30, Sun
9–6

🚌 116 to Piazza della
Rotonda; 30, 40, 46, 62,
63, 64, 70, 81 and all to
Largo di Torre Argentina

♿ Good

✋ Free

❓ Sometimes used for
concerts and special
services

Do not be misled by the inscription, AGRIPPA FECIT, over its
portals. Agrippa built an earlier version of this temple to all
the gods but what we see today was erected by Emperor
Hadrian in the early 1st century AD and, in spite of losing
many of its opulent trimmings over the centuries, it
remains much as he would have remembered it.

The dome is a semi-sphere 43.5m (144ft) in diameter
with walls 6m (18ft) thick, it was constructed by pouring
concrete over a wooden framework. Originally the roof
was covered with bronze cladding which was stripped
off by Constantine II in the 7th century to decorate
Constantinople and, 1,000 years later, Bernini took the
remaining bronze from the roof beams to build the canopy
(*baldacchino*) in St. Peter's (► 26). Its huge bronze doors,
however, have survived since Roman times. The ornate
marble floor is a 19th-century reconstruction of the original
design and the interior has been cleaned and touched up
to restore its subtly vibrant shades.

It was one of the first Roman temples to be converted
into a church (by Pope Boniface IV when Emperor Phocas
donated the building to him; consecrated 609) and over the
centuries several leading Italians, including the painter
Raphael, have been buried here.

6
Piazza Navona

One of the world's most beautiful squares owes its elongated shape to the ancient Roman stadium over which it was built.

Although the best effect can be had by approaching Piazza Navona from the southeast end, whichever of the narrow streets you take, this massive space in the cramped historical centre is always breathtaking. To its north, are remains of the entrance to the stadium that Emperor Domitian built in the 1st century AD.

The piazza's centrepiece is Bernini's spectacular Fontana dei Fiumi (fountain of the rivers, 1651) featuring symbolic representations of the rivers Ganges, Danube, Plate and Nile (blindfolded because its source was then unknown) clinging to a massive artificial cliff-face while sea monsters lurk beneath. The figure at the middle of the fountain to the southeast is another Bernini work, *Il Moro* (the moor); the figures of Neptune and others on the third fountain are 19th-century.

This has always been a hub of Roman social life; there was a market here for centuries and the piazza used to be flooded in August to form a vast watery playground for rich and poor alike. Today it is flooded by musicians, artists, locals and visitors who flock to its bars for hours at a time.

28B3

Piazza Navona

Lots of bars, tend to be expensive but worth it (€€)

40, 46, 62, 64 to Corso Vittorio Emanuele II; 30, 70, 81, 87, 116. 492, 628 to Corso del Rinascimento

December Christmas fair (► 116), street performers all year

Bernini's fountain, topped by an obelisk, reigns over Piazza Navona

7
Roman Forum (Foro Romano)

✝ 28C3

✉ Via dei Fori Imperiali

☎ 06 3996 7700

🕐 9 to 1 hour before sunset

Survey the monumental ruins of Classical Rome

This was the social, economic and political core of ancient Rome, where people came to shop, consult lawyers or gossip.

Before entering the Foro or Forum, look down on it from behind the Campidoglio (➤ 16). To your left is the Arch of Septimius Severus, erected in AD203 to celebrate his victory over the Parthians; behind it, to the right, is the Column of Phocas, AD608, erected in honour of the Byzantine Emperor, Phocas, in gratitude after he gave the Pantheon (➤ 20) to the Pope.

🚇 Colosseo

🚌 75, 85, 117, 175, 810, 850 to Via dei Fori Imperial

♿ Few

🖐 Free

❓ Guided tours available in English

Left of the public entrance to the Forum is the Basilica Aemilia, a place for business; look for traces of the coins that were fused into the floor when the Basilica was burned down in the 5th century. Next to the Basilica, along the Via Sacra (Sacred Way), is the 3rd-century Curia (rebuilt in the 1930s) where the Senate met; the slightly curved platform outside it is the rostrum on which political speeches and orations were made. Opposite the Curia is the 1st-century BC Basilica Julia and to its left is the Temple of Castor and Pollux, with its three beautiful remaining columns. The round building is the Temple of Vesta, where a fire was kept burning continually by the 16 Vestal Virgins who lived in the elegant villa behind it. On the other side of the Forum are the three massive vaults of the 4th-century Basilica of Maxentius and Constantine much studied by Renaissance artists and architects. To its left is the 4th-century AD Temple of Romulus, under which you can see some dank little rooms, thought to be the remains of a much earlier brothel. The Arch of Titus is near the public exit; it was erected in the 1st century AD to celebrate the Emperor's sack of Jerusalem.

8
San Clemente

near Colosseum

A 12th-century church, on top of a 4th-century one, on top of an ancient shrine of Mithras—a walk through Rome's multi-layered history?

Even without its hidden depths, San Clemente is one of the prettiest churches in Rome with its 12th-century apse mosaic, *The Triumph of the Cross*, showing details of animals, birds and humans in flower-filled fields and its simple, 6th-century choir stall, originally in the earlier church building. The spiralling column next to the choir stall is a 12th-century cosmati (➤ 68) mosaic candlestick. To the left of the entrance is the chapel of St. Catherine with 15th-century frescoes by Masolini of her life and martyrdom on the original Catherine-wheel.

However, the church's main claim to fame lies underneath where the first layer comprises the remains of a 4th-century church in which some fragments of ancient masonry and 11th-century frescoes, illustrating the life and miracles of St. Clemente (martyred by being tied to an anchor and drowned), have been preserved among the foundations of the later church. There is also a large circular well that was probably used as a font.

Descending yet further you come to the ancient Roman level where the highlight is a cramped room with a small altar on which there is a relief of Mithras slaying a bull. The Mithraic cult arrived in Rome from Persia about the same time as Christianity and had a strong following especially among soldiers (women were not allowed to join), involving them in ritualistic banquets.

The route out takes you through the walls of several ancient Roman apartment blocks and even lower, although not open to the public, are some 5th or 6th century catacombs.

✝	29D2
✉	Via di San Giovanni in Laterano
☎	06 7045 1018
🕐	Mon–Sat 9–12.30, 3–6, Sun and hols from 10
Ⓜ	Colosseo
🚌	85, 117, 850 to Via di San Giovanni in Laterano; 75, 85, 87, 117, 175 to Piazza del Colosseo
♿	Moderate; free to upper church

View of San Clemente's attractive main façade

9
Sistine Chapel & Vatican Museums

www.vatican.va

73B1

Viale Vaticano

Vatican tourist office: 06 6988 4947. Information on guided tours 06 6988 5100

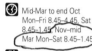
Mid-Mar to end Oct Mon–Fri 8.45–4.45, Sat 8.45–1.45, Nov–mid Mar Mon–Sat 8.45–1.45

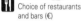
Choice of restaurants and bars (€)

Above: *The prophet Ezekiel, in the Sistine Chapel*
Right: *Michelangelo's masterpiece, covering the ceiling of the Sistine Chapel*

Michelangelo's masterpiece is one of today's wonders of the world, fittingly reached via the rooms of one of the world's greatest art collections.

Before reaching the Sistine Chapel you will have to walk for about 20 minutes through the corridors of the Vatican Museums. There is far too much to be absorbed in one visit, but you can select one of several recommended timed routes to see a selection of the highlights. There are: the Museo Gregoriano-Egizio Egyptian collection; the Museo Chiaramonti collection of Roman sculpture; the Museo Pio Clementine, whose classical sculptures include the *Belvedere Apollo* and *Lacoön* and his sons being strangled by snakes; the Museo Gregoriano-Etrusco collection of Greek, Roman and Etruscan art; corridors of tapestries by Pieter van Aelst based on Raphael cartoons; and corridors lined with 16th-century maps of each of the Italian regions, which lead to the Raphael Rooms.

There are four Raphael Rooms, painted between 1508 and 1525 (the last finished by Giulio Romano after Raphael's death in 1520). In the first room the subjects are metaphysical, including the famous *School of Athens* in which many of Raphael's contemporaries are portrayed as Greek philosophers and poets. The second room shows biblical and early Christian events. The third room portrays significant events in papal history, and the final room illustrates the story of Constantine. From here the tour proceeds to the Sistine Chapel.

Michelangelo painted the Sistine Chapel ceiling between 1508 and 1512, crouching for hours on the scaffolding as Pope Julius II chivvied him on from below. A thorough cleaning in the 1980s and 1990s, during which some of the garments that more puritanical popes had had painted on to Michelangelo's scantily clad biblical figures were stripped off along with the dust and grime, restored the original vibrant hues. The ceiling tells the story of the Creation, in which a pink-clad God nips around dividing light from darkness and water from land before going on to create the sun, the moon, Adam and Eve. The last four panels show the birth of original sin and the story of Noah. On the chapel's end wall is Michelangelo's much later *Last Judgement*. By the time he started this in 1534 he was racked with ill-health and pessimistic thoughts of his own mortality, and it took him until 1541 to complete. The flayed skin held up by St. Bartholomew (to Christ's left) is believed to be a self-portrait, while the diabolical figure in the bottom right-hand corner is a portrait of the Pope's secretary, who disapproved of Michelangelo's naturalistic handling of this sacred subject. The other walls of the chapel were painted with episodes from the lives of Christ and Moses by, among others, Botticelli, and Perugino.

Beyond the chapel are: the Vatican library with over one million valuable volumes, many dating from the Middle Ages; a gallery of modern religious art including works by Klee, Munch and Picasso; and collections of pagan and early Christian antiquities. It is definitely worth going into the *Pinacoteca* (picture gallery) which has a marvellous collection of medieval, Renaissance and baroque art including masterpieces by most of the most famous names in European art of the periods.

Ottaviano

23, 32, 49, 81, 492, 990, to Piazza del Risorgimento

Good

Expensive but it covers a lot; free last Sun of month

Guided tours available in a number of languages. It is quieter to visit in the afternoon and best to avoid Saturdays

10
St. Peter's (San Pietro)

www.vatican.va

✝ 73B1

✉ Piazza San Pietro

☎ 06 6988 1662

🕐 Apr–end Sep daily 7–7;
Oct–end Mar 7–6

Ⓜ Ottaviano

🚌 64 to Piazza San Pietro;
23, 32, 49, 81, 492, 990
to Piazza del
Risorgimento

✋ Free to Basilica; elevator
or stairs moderate to
roof

❓ Tours of the necropolis
in English must be
booked in advance
through the Uffizio degli
Scavi in St. Peter's
Square.

*Looking down from the
dome designed by
Michelangelo*

*Whether you find its opulence impressive or over
the top, the sheer size of the world's most
important church will not leave you unmoved*

Emperor Constantine built a shrine to St. Peter over his
tomb and near where he had been crucified in the Circus
of Nero. As the fortunes of Rome and the newly established Christian religion rose and fell, the building saw
periods of embellishment fluctuating with sackings and
destruction, and had been much altered by the time Pope
Nicholas V ordered its restoration in the mid-15th century.
Work did not get under way until about 50 years later,
however, when Pope Julius II appointed Bramante as the
architect for a completely new basilica in 1503. Another
123 years, and interventions from many of the most
important architects and artists of the time, were to pass
before the new basilica was consecrated. The basic floor
plan is as Bramante designed it, 187m (613ft) long;
Michelangelo designed the 132.5-m (435-ft) high dome,
Carlo Maderno the façade and Bernini the impressive oval
colonnade that surrounds the piazza in front of the basilica.

Inside, on the right, is Michelangelo's *Pietà* of 1499.
Other gems include a 13th-century bronze statue of St.
Peter whose foot has been worn away by the touch of
pilgrims; Bernini's massive 20-m (66-ft) high *baldacchino*,
or altar canopy (under which only the Pope can celebrate
Mass), his monuments to Popes Urban VIII and Alexander
VII and the tabernacle in the shape of a temple.

What To See

Rome   30–79
In the Know   34–35
Food and Drink   50–51
Excursions from the City   80–90

Above: *Dome of St. Peter's Basilica*
Right: *Detail from the Sistine Chapel ceiling*

27

CENTRAL ROME

7 Hotel

Rome

Rome has been a major city for longer than most other European capitals have existed. First the heart of the Roman Empire, a few centuries later it emerged as the centre of the Roman Catholic faith and finally, in 1870, it became the capital of the newly united Italy. In Rome's museums you can see artworks and artefacts from well over 2,000 years of history—exquisite ancient sculptures, delicate early Renaissance and opulent baroque paintings and much more. Sightseers' Rome breaks into two sections, ancient and Renaissance-baroque, but wherever you are you're likely to suddenly come across some remnant from centuries earlier than its surroundings.

Add the plethora of cool bars, ice-cream shops and restaurants as well as boutiques that attract the fashion-conscious and you've got a place that can guarantee a wonderful visit.

'At each step, a palace, a ruin, a garden, a desert, a little house, a stable, a triumphal arch, a colonnade, and all these so close together that one could draw them on a small sheet of paper.'

J. W. VON GOETHE
The Italian Journey (1786–8)

The City of Rome

Rome is an ideal city for sightseeing. Nearly all of the main monuments, museums and churches are within walking distance of each other and wherever you look, you are likely to come across some picturesque detail (flower-filled balconies, pristine shirts and sheets hanging out to dry, sleepy cats snoozing on car bonnets (hoods), ruined splendour, a little shrine with a portrait of the Madonna and perhaps even a candle) that is guaranteed to charm anybody used to more severe northern cities.

Mornings are the best times for catching opening hours; most churches and museums close at lunchtime and some, but by no means all, reopen at about 4 or 5pm. In summer the middle of the day tends to be too hot for sightseeing anyway so you can use this time for a rest or a leisurely lunch under the awnings of an outdoor restaurant.

The Vatican City, here viewed from across the Tiber, is the world's smallest independent sovereign state, and also the most ancient

What to See in Rome

28C3
Piazza dell'Accademia di San Luca 77
06 679 8850
Mon–Sat 10–12.30
Barberini
52, 53, 61, 62, 63, 71, 95, 116, 119, 175, 492, 630 to Via del Tritone
Few
Free

ACCADEMIA DI SAN LUCA ✪

Rome's academy of fine arts was founded by Pope Gregory XIII in 1577. It moved to its present site, the Palazzo Carpegna, in the 1930s when its previous home was cleared to make way for Via dei Fori Imperiali. The building has an unusual inclined spiral ramp (designed by Borromini), instead of stairs, to the upper levels. The collection is predominantly the work of academicians, or was presented by them, with plenty of fine portraits and still lifes. Highlights include a fresco fragment by Raphael, three works attributed to Titian, and paintings by Guido Reni, Van Dyck and Angelica Kauffman, one of the few women members of the academy.

73C2
Viale Vaticano
06 6988 4947/6988 3333
Easter to mid-Jun Mon–Fri 8.45–3.45, Sat 8.45–1.45. Rest of year, Mon–Sat 8.45–1.45. All year, last Sun of month 8.45–1.45pm
Ottaviano
23, 32, 49, 81, 492, 990, to Piazza del Risorgimento
Expensive but covers all Vatican museums

APPARTAMENTO BORGIO ✪

This suite of apartments within the Vatican Museums (► 24) was built for Pope Alexander VI, a member of the notorious Borgia family, during his papacy (1492–1503). Almost a palace within a palace, it proved so sumptious that subsequent popes chose to use it as their principal lodgings for the next hundred years. Room 1, the Sala delle Sibille, is where the infamous Cesare Borgia is said to have had Alfonso of Aragon, the husband of his sister, Lucretia Borgia, murdered. Today the room is more remarkable for its frescoes executed between 1492 and 1495 by Umbrian artist Pinturicchio .

28C4
Via di Ripeta
06 6880 6848
Temporarily closed for restoration; check with tourist office

ARA PACIS AUGUSTAE ✪✪

A modern glass pavilion on the banks of the Tiber houses some of the finest Roman sculpture to have survived. The Ara Pacis (altar of peace) was commissioned by the Senate in 13BC to celebrate the victories of Emperor Augustus in Spain and Gaul; the outer walls of the enclosure that surrounds it depict a procession in which the faces of the imperial family and other important Romans can be seen. The panels by the entrances represent some symbolic moments from the history and mythology of Rome. Behind the altar is the round mausoleum of Augustus, built by the forward-planning emperor in 28BC, 42 years before his death.

A marble relief depicting the earth goddess Tellus with animals at her feet

ARCO DI COSTANTINO ✪✪

Although known as Constantine's Arch, scholars now believe that this magnificent monument outside the Colosseum was originally built in honour of the emperor, Trajan, and adopted by Constantine who made a few alterations and rededicated it to his own triumph over co-emperor Maxentius in AD315. In any event, many of the carved panels and medallions were scavenged from older monuments, including the figures of Dacian prisoners at the top of the columns, which were almost certainly carved for Trajan.

🕂 29D2
✉ Piazza del Colosseo
Ⓜ Colosseo
🚌 60, 75, 81, 85, 87, 117, 175 to Piazza del Colosseo
✋ Free

BASILICA DI SAN GIOVANNI E PAOLO ✪✪

Archaeology meets legend in this church, built over a two-storey Roman house, and containing Roman and medieval frescoes (seen by appointment only). Saints John and Paul were martyred here in 362, and their bodies, discovered only in the 20th century, are now in an ancient porphyry urn under the altar. The inside was modelled in 1718. There is a 13th-century fresco in a small room near the altar which depicts Christ and his Apostles. The church itself is predominantly Byzantine and has one of the most beautiful belltowers in Rome (1150), which was added by the only English pope, Nicholas Breakspeake (Adrian IV) as well as a majestic portico incorporating ancient columns.

🕂 29D3
✉ Piazza dei Santi Giovanni e Paolo 13
☎ 06 7005 745
🕐 8.30–12, 3–6.30
Ⓜ Colosseo
🚌 81, 673 to Via della Navicella

Arco di Costantino, like most monuments in Rome, is built in travertine, a white stone from Tivoli

33

In the Know

If you only have a short time to visit Rome, or would like to get a real flavour of the city, here are some ideas:

10
Ways To Be A Local

Learn a few phrases in Italian for a wonderfully appreciative response.
Be an assertive pedestrian; Roman drivers may look like maniacs but they can have lightning quick reactions and stop if you look determined to cross the road. Make sure you choose a spot where drivers will see you in time, however, and do not take any chances.
Dress comfortably but not scruffily; whether you like the style or not, Italians are nearly always well turned out.
Women, do not be offended by what you may see as invasive male attention—be politely assertive if you do not reciprocate the interest.
Relax; walk at a dignified, leisurely pace. Never rush.
Try not to drink cappuccino after dinner.

Eat ice-cream in the street, but nothing else.
Jaywalk; never use pavements when you can stroll down the middle of the cobbled street.
Do not get drunk. Italians seldom do.

10
Top Places To Have Lunch

Antica Birreria Fratelli Tempera (€) ⊠ Via San Marcello 19 ☎ 06 678 6203. Ideal for a simple lunch. Original art nouveau interior and a large beer hall.
Binario 4 (➤ 93).
Cecilia Metella (➤ 93).
Enoteca Corsi (➤ 94).
Frontoni (€) ⊠ Viale Trastevere 52–8 ☎ 06 581 2436. A massive range of fillings from which to invent your own pizza.
Insalata Ricca (€) ⊠ Piazza di Pasquino 72, and ⊠ Largo dei Chiavari 8 ☎ 06 6880 3656. Light pasta dishes and big, meal-in-themselves salads.

Lorodinapoli (➤ 95).
News Café (➤ 95)
Panattoni (➤ 96).
Il Margutta (➤ 95).

5
Best Views

- Gianicolo (➤ 43).
- Palatino (➤ 52).
- Pincio, Villa Borghese (➤ 12).
- Ponte Garibaldi
- St. Peter's roof (➤ 26).

10
Top Activities

Explore: hire a *motorino* (scooter) ⊠ Bike e Scooter Rental, via Cavour 80a ☎ 06 481 5669.
Beach: Spend a day at the beach (➤ 115).
Football (soccer): go to a football match (➤ 115).
Concerts and films: go to an outdoor concert or film-screening (➤ 112).
Historic centre: spend half a day wandering around the historic centre, *without a guide book*, or in one of the parks (➤ 58).
Lunch: spend all afternoon having lunch (see list above or ➤ 92–99 for ideas).
The Pope: attend the Pope's blessing. The Pope addresses the crowds in St. Peter's Square from his apartments on Sunday mornings.

A civilized lunch is important to Romans

Campo de' Fiori Market; romantic Pincio Hill

Coffee: have a really good coffee ✉ Bar Sant'Eustachio, Piazza Sant'Eustachio 82, ☎ 06 6880 2048).

Markets: spend a Sunday morning at Porta Portese flea market, or wander round another of the markets listed (➤ 109).

Window shop, or buy, in the designer area around Via Condotti (➤ 77).

5
Best Ice-Creams

• Giolitti (€) ✉ Via Uffici del Vicario 40 ☎ 06 699 1243. Wide range of flavours.
• Da Mirella (€) ✉ Lungotevere Anguillara, Ponte Cestio. *Grattacheccha* (grated ice served with flavoured syrups or juice) during the summer.
• Il Palazzo del Freddo (€) ✉ Via Principe Eugenio 65–7 ☎ 06 446 4740. Hundreds of different chilled desserts.
• Gelateria della Palma (€) ✉ Via della Maddelena 20. Over 100 flavours.
• Tre Scalini (€) ✉ Piazza Navona 28–32 ☎ 06 6880 1996. Rich chocolate *tartufi*.

10
Best Churches

• Gesù (➤ 43), for baroque opulence.
• Sant'Andrea al Quirinale (➤ 63), for Bernini.
• San Clemente (➤ 23), for history.
• San Giovanni in Laterano (➤ 65), for history.
• Santa Maria in Domnica (➤ 69), for mosaics.
• Santa Maria Maggiore (➤ 36), for mosaics and history.
• Santa Maria sopra Minerva (➤ 69), for art and originality (a Gothic church, rare for Rome).
• Santa Maria del Popolo (➤ 70), for art.
• Santa Maria in Trastevere (➤ 70) for mosaics.
• St. Peter's (➤ 26), for size, importance and everything else. .

35

29D3
Piazza di Santa Maria
Maggiore
06 483195
7–6.45
Termini, Cavour
16, 70, 71, 75, 84, 360 to
Largo di Torre Argentina

Lavish mosaics at
Basilica di San Paolo
Fuori le Mura

BASILICA DI SANTA MARIA MAGGIORE ✪✪✪

On entering you are confronted by the seemingly endless rows of the nave's columns, the sweep of the cosmati floor and a ceiling decorated with the first gold to be brought from the New World. The Sistine (1585) and Pauline (1611) side chapels have opulent works by the most important artists of the day (Maderno, Reni and Ponzio to name but a few). The mosaics are, however, the basilica's glory. On the nave, a 5th-century narrative of the Old Testament and, in the apse, a stunning Glorification of Mary (1295) to whom the church is dedicated, Our Lady herself indicating the site by sending the sign of snowfall in August, an event still celebrated every year. The façade (1743–50) has been restored to its colourful magnificence.

www.abbaziasanpaolo.net
Off map at 28C1
Via Ostiense 186
06 541 0341
7–6; cloisters 9–1, 3–6
San Paolo
128, 761, 770 to San
Paolo Basilica

BASILICA DI SAN PAOLO FUORI LE MURA ✪✪

Built on the site of St. Paul's execution (c67), the present basilica dates from 1874 (Poletti), the original (c386–410) having burnt down in 1823. The only surviving parts are in the transept, the bronze doors (1070), an impressive example of a paschal candlestick (c1190), Arnolfo di Cambio's lovely Gothic *baldacchino* (1285) and the beautiful cloisters (1205–41) with their lavishly decorated mosaic columns (1214, Vassallettis). The general tone, however, is somewhat heavy-handed and 19th-century.

Off map at 29D1
Via Appia Antica 136
06 780 8847
Fri–Wed 9–12, 2.30–5
118, 660 to San
Sebastiano

BASILICA DI SAN SEBASTIANO ✪

The basilica dates from the first half of the 5th century, on the spot where Peter and Paul's bodies were allegedly buried (their names can be seen in the graffiti on the walls of the catacombs beneath)—the present building dates from the early 17th century. The burial chambers (entered on the left of the façade) also contain exquisite Roman frescoes and stucco work. In pride of place, however, is the crypt of St. Sebastian, whose image, pierced by the Diocletian guards' arrows, was particularly popular during the Renaissance. His body lies in the calm white-walled basilica above.

CAMPIDOGLIO (► 16, TOP TEN)

CAMPO DE' FIORI ✪✪✪

Since Renaissance times, this has been one of the most bustling, busiest squares in central Rome and is still a great place to drop by at any time of day. Many of the old, crumbling buildings have been restored but the fascinatingly precarious many-layered Palazzo Pio Righetti, set at the square's northeastern corner, still looks as though one of its plant-covered balconies may be about to drop off. During the morning there is a colourful food market which packs up noisily as people saunter to the outdoor restaurants and bars at lunchtime. The foreboding, hooded figure in the middle of the piazza is Giordano Bruno, a philosopher who was burnt at the stake here in 1600 for heresy—the statue was erected when the popes lost their political control of Rome at Italian Unification. The maze of narrow streets that surround the piazza are full of carpenters' and jewellers' workshops, antique and second-hand clothing shops.

🕂 28C3
✉ Piazza Campo de' Fiori
🚌 40, 46, 62, 64 to Corso Vittorio Emaneule

Campo de' Fiori translates as 'field of flowers'; today its market is full of fruit and vegetables

CASTEL SANT'ANGELO (► 17, TOP TEN)

CATACOMBS OF SAN CALLISTO ✪

In ancient Rome, when Christianity was still very much a minority religion, it was against the law to bury the dead within the city confines. The catacombs of San Callisto, set in rolling parkland off the Via Appia Antica, are among the largest and most visited. Here there are thought to be a total of 20km (12 miles) of underground galleries on four levels lined with niches, or *loculi*, cut into the rock in which the shrouded bodies of the dead were laid to rest behind stone. Many of the early popes were buried here. The guided tours (offered in a range of languages including English, French and German) cover about 1km (half a mile).

www.catacombe.roma.it
🕂 29D1
✉ Via Appia Antica 110
☎ 06 5130 1580
🕐 Thu–Tue 8.30–12, 2.30–5.30. Closed Feb
🚌 118, 660 to San Callisto
♿ Moderate

www.catacombedipriscilla.com

✚ Off map at 29E5
✉ Via Salaria 430
☎ 06 8620 6272
🕐 Tue–Sun 8.30–12, 2.30–5. Closed Jan
🚌 63, 92, 310 to Santa Priscilla
👆 Moderate

✚ 28B3
✉ Piazza della Chiesa Nuova
🕐 7–12, 4–7
🚌 40, 46, 62, 64 to Piazza della Chiesa Nuova

CATACOMBS OF SANTA PRISCILLA

These are probably the most charming of Rome's many catacomb complexes, in the Trieste area, northeast of the centre. The guided tour of the 50-m (164-ft) deep galleries, where 40,000 early Christians were laid to rest, is led by polyglot nuns and includes the earliest-known picture of the Virgin (2nd century AD) and a chapel with frescoes of bible stories. Priscilla was the widow of a Christian who was martyred by Emperor Domitian; the catacombs were dug under the foundations of Priscilla's house.

CHIESA NUOVA 🟢

This was one of the churches which helped to transform the face of Rome in the Catholic resurgence of the 17th century. It is the seat of one of the most important Counter-Reformatory movements, St. Phillip Neri's Oratorians. He originally wanted the nave simply white-washed but did not reckon on the exuberant baroque fresco cycles that were to make their dazzling mark in Roman churches half a century later. The breath-taking example here is Pietro di Cortona's (on the nave ceiling, dome and apse, 1647–56). Next door is the brilliant Borromini's superb Oratory façade (1637–40), which is cunningly detailed.

Did you know ?

Filippo Neri (1515–95), the founder of the Oratorian order for whom Chiesa Nuova was built, was a Florentine banker who had a sudden conversion to Christianity and came to Rome. The emphasis he put on helping the poor, sick, old and young helped him to attract many followers, even though he is said to have made the richer ones humble themselves by dressing in rags.

The Chiesa Nuova set the style for Roman churches in the 17th century

CIRCO MASSIMO ✪✪✪

SW of Colosseum Nr Palatine

There is not much of this ancient racetrack left but you can make out the tight oval that the charioteers careered round and the sloped side on which there was tiered seating for up to 300,000 spectators. The remains of that seating can still be seen at the circus's southern end, although the tower there is medieval. Chariot races were held here from the 4th century BC until they went out of fashion in the 6th century AD. The site was also used for wild-animal fights, mock sea battles (for which it was flooded), athletics and mass executions.

✛ 28C2
✉ Via del Circo Massimo
Ⓜ Circo Massimo
🚌 60, 75, 81, 160, 175, 628, 673 to Piazza di Porta Capena
♿ Possible
Ⓜ Free

COLOSSEUM (COLOSSEO) (➤ 18, TOP TEN)

COLUMN OF MARCUS AURELIUS ✪

Nr Trevi Fountain

In the square outside Palazzo Chigi, the prime minister's official residence, and the offices of newspaper *Il Tempo*, is an intricately carved column erected in honour of Emperor Marcus Aurelius after his death in AD 180. It is about 30m (98ft) high and depicts scenes from the Emperor's successful German campaign. The statue of St. Paul at the top of the column replaced the original of Marcus Aurelius on the orders of Pope Sixtus V in 1588.

✛ 28C3
✉ Piazza Colonna
🚌 62, 63, 81, 85, 95, 117, 119 and services to Via del Corso

DOMUS AUREA ✪✪

Reopened to the public in 1999, after nearly 20 years of restoration, the Domus Aurea is Emperor Nero's 'Golden House'. After the great fire of AD64 destroyed over half the city (and when Nero acquired his fiddling reputation), he built this huge symbol of Imperial power over the ruins. It is adorned with elegant fresco cycles and paintings. Tickets must be booked in advance.

✛ 29D3
✉ Via della Domus Aurea, Colle Oppio
☎ 06 3996 7700
🕐 Wed–Mon 9–7
Ⓜ Colosseo
🚌 60, 75, 84, 85, 87, 117, 175, 810, 850 to Colosseo
Ⓜ Moderate

FONTANA DELLE TARTARUGHE ✪✪

This delightfully delicate fountain, in Piazza Mattei, showing four male nymphs with tantalisingly enigmatic smiles cavorting provocatively around its edges, was the work of Giacomo della Porta and Taddeo Landini in the 1580s. The contrastingly precarious tortoises are believed to have been added by Bernini in the following century. According to legend the fountain was erected overnight by the Duke of Mattei who wanted to show his potential father-in-law that he was still capable of achieving great things even though he had just lost his fortune. He also had one of the windows of his palace blocked up so that nobody else would ever see it from that superb vantage point.

✛ 28C3
✉ Piazza Mattei
🚌 30, 70, 81, 87, 116 to Largo di Torre Argentina

The beautiful Fontana delle Tartarughe is a landmark in one of the most elegant squares in central Rome

🔲 28C3
✉ Piazza di Trevi
🚌 52, 53, 61, 62, 71, 81, 95, 117, 119 and other routes to Via del Tritone and Via del Corso

Below: *Remains of smaller forums alongside the Roman Forum;*
Opposite: *The Fontana di Trevi is a must for anyone's agenda*

FONTANA DI TREVI ✪✪✪

Even without Anita Ekberg, famous for the *Dolce Vita* scene in which she immerses herself in its turbulent waters, this effusively over-the-top fountain is a must for any visitor to Rome (and anyone with any intention of returning to the city should make sure they throw a coin into it). It was designed by Nicolò Salvi in 1762 and shows Neptune flanked by two massive steeds representing the calm and stormy sea bursting out of an artificial cliff-face which contrasts beautifully with the calm orderliness of the Palazzo Poli in whose wall it is built. The panels across the top depict the finding of the spring that feeds the ancient Roman canal leading into the fountain. By the way, the water is now said to contain bleach.

🔲 28C3
✉ Via dei Fori Imperiali
☎ 06 679 0048
🕐 Tue–Sun 9–6.30 (until 4.30 Nov–end Mar)
Ⓜ Colosseo
🚌 60, 84, 85, 87, 117, 175, 810, 850 to Via dei Fori Imperiali
💵 Expensive

FORI IMPERIALI ✪✪

Opposite and next to the main Roman Forum (➤ 22) lie the remaining fragments of five other, smaller, forums each built by an emperor to accommodate the overspill when the original forum became too small to cope with the demands of an expanding empire. To the right of the main entrance to the Roman Forum, underneath the Vittorio Emanuele Monument (➤ 46) is the oldest of these, built by Julius Caesar in AD51; on the other side of the wide avenue that Mussolini built over other ancient remains to act as a triumphal route up to his Palazzo Venezia headquarters (➤ 56) are the remains of the forums of Trajan (Mercati Traianei ➤ 46), Augustus (where you can see some fine columns and friezes), Vespasian and Nerva.

THE FORUM (FORO ROMANO) (► 22, TOP TEN)

GALLERIA BORGHESE   ✪✪✪

29D4

✉ Piazzale del Museo Borghese 5

☎ 06 841 7645

🕐 Tue–Sun 9–7

🍴 Bar

Ⓜ Spagna/Flamino

🚌 52, 53, 910 to Via Pinciana

💷 Expensive

❓ Advance reservations necessary

Canova's reclining Paolina Bonaparte Borghese

Finally, after years of restoration work, the whole gallery (both sculpture and painting sections) reopened in summer 1997. The sculpture collection, on the ground floor, includes some important classical works, such as a *Sleeping Hermaphrodite* and a *Dancing Faun*, and the famous Canova sculpture of Paolina Bonaparte Borghese as a reclining Venus. The highlights, however, are the spectacular sculptures by Bernini. Cardinal Scipione Borghese, who had the villa and park built between 1608 and 1615, was Bernini's first patron. Here the sculptor's precocious talent is evident in works such as *The Rape of Proserpine, David* (thought to be a self-portrait) and *Daphne and Apollo*. The paintings are on the ground-floor walls and upstairs. Among the celebrated works are a *Deposition* by Raphael, Titian's early masterpiece, *Sacred and Profane Love*, a restored *Last Supper* by Jacopo Bassano, now rich and vibrant, Correggio's erotic *Danae*, and fine works by Guercino, Veronese, Giorgione and Andrea del Sarto. Caravaggio is represented here by six paintings, including one of his most important early works, the luscious *Boy with a Fruit Basket*, the *Sick Bacchus* and also the wonderfully realistic *Madonna of the Serpent*.

GALLERIA NAZIONALE D'ARTE MODERNA E CONTEMPORANEA   ✪

28C5

✉ Viale delle Belle Arti 131

☎ 06 322981

🕐 Tue–Sun 8.30–7.30

🚋 Trams 19, 30B to Viale delle Belle Arti

💷 Expensive

↔ Villa Giulia (► 78)

Cesare Bazzini's *Belle Epoque* palace is one of the few remaining buildings erected for the Rome International Exhibition of 1911 in the northwest area of the park of Villa Borghese. The collection covers the 19th and 20th centuries, mostly Italian artists—De Chirico, the Futurists and the *macchiaioli* (Italy's answer to the French Impressionists)—although there are also works by Gustav Klimt, Paul Cézanne and Henry Moore. Major temporary exhibitions are also staged. The museum has been extensively renovated, long-closed wings are being opened up, there is a new sculpture section, and important contemporary acquisitions have been made.

IL GESÙ ✪✪

This church spans the whole of the baroque: from the floor plan (by Vignola, 1568, and probably based on the ideas of one of Michelangelo's last architectural plans), through the façade (with its triangular pediment and side scrolls) and dome (by Giacomo della Porta, 1575) to Pietro da Cortona's altar of St. Xavier (1674) and Andrea Pozzo's almost vulgarly ornate chapel of St. Ignatius (1696). This is the central church of the Jesuits, the severe order founded by Ignatius Loyola in the 16th century—its design has been imitated in Jesuit church-building all over the world. Next door are the rooms occupied by Loyola (usually open when the church is) which have a wonderful *trompe l'oeil* fresco by Pozzo.

🔲 28C3
✉ Piazza del Gesù
☎ 06 6970 0232
🕐 6–12.30, 4–7.15
🚌 40, 46, 62, 63, 64, 70, 81 and services to Largo di Torre Argentina

THE GHETTO ✪✪

The Jewish community in Rome is one of the oldest in Europe and dates from the 1st century BC, although it first settled this area north of Isola Tiberina (➤ 45) in the 13th century. From the mid-16th century until Italian Unification in 1870 Roman Jews were enclosed behind high walls in this warren of narrow, winding alleyways which still house kosher butchers, excellent Jewish restaurants and a baker offering Roman Jewish specialities such as *torta di ricotta* and sweet 'pizzas' made with candied and dried fruit. At the heart of the ghetto was the old fish market held in front of the Portico d'Ottavia, the only remains of a vast shop and temple complex, which was renovated in the 1st century BC and named in honour of Emperor Augustus's sister Octavia.

🔲 28C3
✉ Via del Portico d'Ottavia (and the streets north)
🚌 H, 8, 63, 630, 780 to Via Arenula

Below: *Gianicolo hill takes its name from the god Janus*

GIANICOLO ✪✪

The hill that rises between Trastevere and the Vatican to the southwest of the Tiber has some of the best views of central Rome and is a popular lovers' tryst. At its summit is Piazza Giuseppe Garibaldi, where a rousing equestrian statue of Giuseppe Garibaldi commemorates his 1849 victory over the French here when he led the troops of the Roman Republic in the struggle for Italian unification.

🔲 28B3
✉ Passeggiata del Gianicolo
🚌 870 to Passeggiata del Gianicolo

Gianicolo to the Ghetto

Distance
4km (2.5 miles)

Time
2 hours, or 4 with stops for
coffee and visits

Start point
Piazza Garibaldi
🕀 28B3
🚌 41

End point
The Ghetto
🕀 28C3
🚌 44

Lunch
La Taverna del Ghetto (€)
(➤ 98)
✉ Via Porteico d'Ottavia 8
☎ 06 6880 9771

The church of San
Bartolomeo stands on the
tiny Isola Tiberina

Start at Piazza Garibaldi on the Gianicolo (➤ 43).

*Follow the road southeast, past the busts of
heroes of the Risorgimento, to the gateway, turn
left down the staircase.*

But first look at the monumental baroque Fontana Paola,
where people once washed their clothes.

*Follow the road down past the Spanish
Embassy and turn left on Via Garibaldi. Go to
the bottom where, to the left, is Porta Settimiana
(1498), the gateway pilgrims used to reach the
Vatican. Turn right down Via della Scala.*

The church of Santa Maria della Scala dates from the late
16th century. Its plain façade hides a rich, cluttered interior.

*Continue into Piazza San Egidio, past the
Museo di Roma in Trastevere (➤ 48), and go
left, passing Vicolo del Piede into Piazza Santa
Maria in Trastevere.*

Here are the church (➤ 70), with its 12th-century mosaics
on the façade, and fountain by Carlo Fontana (1692).

*Continue straight through the piazza and follow
Via della Lungaretta to Piazza Sonnino.*

On the right is the 12th-century bell tower of the ancient
church of San Crisogono, rebuilt in the 16th century.

*Cross the piazza. The left-corner tower is 13th-
century and home to the Dante Society. Go on to
Piazza di Piscinula, turn left up a staircase
along the side of an old palace and cross the
Lungotevere to get to Isola Tiberina (➤ 45).*

Isola Tiberina somewhat resembles a ship and was a
strategic point in ancient times being one of the few points
at which the Tiber could be easily crossed.

*Cross the island to the Ghetto (➤ 43); on the
right is the Synagogue (1874). Straight ahead
the Via Portico d'Ottavia is a good lunch stop.*

ISOLA TIBERINA

From the right-hand (Ghetto-) side of the river, Isola Tiberina is reached via the oldest original bridge over the Tiber, the Ponte Fabricio (62BC). Originally the walls of the buildings rose directly out of the river but, since the end of the 19th century, the island has been surrounded by a wide embankment, now a popular spot for taking early-season sun. The church of San Bartolomeo was built in the 10th century on the site of a 3rd-century BC temple to the god of healing, Aesculapius, and the connection with health has been continued by the Fatebenefratelli hospital which now covers most of the island. Downstream you can see the one remaining arch of the Ponte Rotto (broken bridge) which was the first stone bridge in Rome (142BC), although it had already fallen down at least twice before this mid-16th-century rebuild collapsed in 1598.

28C2
Isola Tiberina
H, 23, 63, 280 to Lungotevere dei Cenci or to Lungotevere Anguillara

The Landmark Trust
This charity rescues buildings, and lets them out for holidays. When the Keats-Shelley Memorial Association launched an appeal for funds to maintain the Keats-Shelley Memorial House, the Trust took on the 3rd-floor flat, restoring it to its appearance in about 1800. The sitting room overlooks the Spanish Steps. Handbook and prices from: The Landmark Trust, Shottesbrooke, Maidenhead, Berkshire SL6 3SW, UK (☎ 01628 825925).

KEATS-SHELLEY MEMORIAL HOUSE

Since 1909 the house at the foot of the Spanish Steps, where Keats died of consumption aged only 25 in February 1821, has been a memorial to Keats, Shelley, Byron and other romantic poets. The rooms which Keats occupied on the first floor now contain a collection of manuscripts, documents and ephemera including Keats's death mask and a lock of his hair. There is also an extensive specialist library. There is a **Landmark Trust** flat on the 3rd floor.

www.keats-shelley-house.org
28C4
Piazza di Spagna 26
06 678 4235
Mon–Fri 9–1, 3–6, Sat 11–4, 3–6
Spagna
119 to Piazza di Spagna
Inexpensive; maximum of 15 at one time

LARGO ARGENTINA

Behind one of the busiest bus intersections in the Area Sacra at Largo Argentina are the remains of four Republican-era temples, known as temples A, B, C and D (in alphabetical order starting nearest the main bus stop). Temple C is the oldest (4th century BC) while 3rd-century BC Temple A was used as a church during the Middle Ages (remains of two apses); behind it are the drains of a massive public toilet. Julius Caesar was murdered near here in 44BC when the Senate were using the Curia of Pompey as a temporary meeting place while the main senate house was being restored. The area is rarely open to the public.

28C3
Largo di Torre Argentina
Some evenings in summer for guided tours in English and Italian
40, 46, 62, 63, 64, 70, 81, 492, 628, 780, 916 to Largo di Torre Argentina

Right: *This statue stands before the Vittorio Emanuele Monument, built to celebrate the first King of Unified Italy*

➕ 28C3
✉ Clivo Argentario 1, Via di San Pietro in Carcere
☎ 06 679 2902
🕐 Apr–end Sep 9–12, 2–6.30; Oct–end Mar 9–12.30, 2.30– 5
🚌 44, 46, 84, 715, 716, 780, 781, 810, 916 to Piazza Venezia 🐾 Donation

➕ 28C3
✉ Via IV Novembre 94
☎ 06 679 0048
🕐 Apr–end Sep Tue–Sun 9–6.30; Oct–end Mar Tue–Sun 9–4.30
🚌 40, 60, 64, 70, 117, 170, H to Via IV Novembre
♿ Limited
🐾 Expensive

➕ 28C3
✉ Piazza Venezia
☎ 06 699 1718
🕐 Apr–end Mar 9.30–5.30, Oct–end Mar 9.30–4.30
🚌 44, 46, 84, 715, 716, 780, 781, 810, 916 to Piazza Venezia
♿ None
🐾 Free

➕ Off map south`
✉ Viale Lincoln 3, EUR
☎ 06 5422 8199

MAMERTINE PRISON (CARCERE MAMERTINO) ✪

This dank, dark dungeon dates from the 4th century BC and was where any potential threats to state security, including the leaders of opposing armies, were thrown to starve to death (their bodies were dropped into the main sewer, the Cloaca Maxima). St. Peter is said to have been imprisoned here before being crucified and an altar has been built next to the spring that he miraculously created in order to christen other prisoners and two of his guards.

MERCATI TRAIANO ✪✪

One of the first shopping malls in the world, Emperor Trajan commissioned this five-level complex of about 150 small shops from the Greek architect Apollodorus of Damascus in the early 2nd century AD. Goods from all over the empire were sold here and shops were probably arranged by area—storage jars found on the first floor suggest that wine and oil were sold here while fruit and flower shops probably occupied the ground floor. The finely carved column next to the markets was erected in AD113 to celebrate Trajan's campaigns in Dacia (Romania). It is 40m (131ft) high and originally bore a statue of the emperor which was replaced by the present St. Peter in 1587.

MONUMENTO A VITTORIO EMANUELE II ✪✪

A monument of many names; *il Vittoriale* was built at the end of the 19th century to honour the first king of the united Italy whose equestrian statue stands out proudly in front. Behind him burns the eternal flame guarded day and night by armed soldiers at the Altar of the Nation while other, less complimentary, ways of referring to this colon-naded mass of white marble include the 'typewriter' and the 'wedding cake'. In any event, you cannot miss it.

MUSEO DELL'ALTO MEDIOEVO ✪

This museum houses decorative arts of the 5th to 11th centuries (from the fall of the Roman Empire to the Renaissance). Most of the artefacts were found locally, and include some beautiful jewellery from the 7th century, fragments of elaborate embroidery from clerical robes and a delicate 5th-century gold fibula found on the Palatine hill. Swords made from gold and silver, intricately carved and decorated, demonstrate how objects made from pure metals can withstand the test of time better than more reactive ones.

MUSEO DELLE ARTI E TRADIZIONI POPOLARI ✪

A huge collection of fascinating objects relating to Italian folk art and rural traditions. On display are agricultural and pastoral tools, including elaborately decorated carts and horse tack, artisan instruments and handiwork, clothing, furniture, musical instruments, some exquisite traditional jewellery and photographs documenting how the exhibits were used.

🕐 Tue–Sun 9–8
Ⓜ Magliana
🚌 714, 715 to Piazzale G
   Marconi
💶 Inexpensive

www.popolari.arti.
benicultural.it
➕ Off map south
✉ Piazza G Marconi 8, EUR
☎ 06 592 6148
🕐 Tue–Sun 9–8
Ⓜ Magliana
🚌 714, 715
💶 Moderate

MUSEO BARRACCO ✪

www.comune.roma.it/
museobarracco
📫 28B3
✉ Corso Vittorio Emanuele
II 168
☎ 06 6880 6848
🕐 Temporarily closed for
restoration; check with
tourist office.

This is one of Rome's most charming museums but often overlooked. The exquisite, small collection of Assyrian, Egyptian, Greek and Roman sculptures (including a series of Roman heads minus their noses) and artefacts was created by Senator Giovanni Barracco and presented to the city in 1902. Underneath the museum (ask the attendants to take you down) are remains of what is said to be a Roman fish shop, complete with counter and a water trough. Fresco fragments (from the 4th century AD) found there are displayed on the ground floor.

MUSEO DELLA CIVILTÀ ROMANA ✪

www.comune.roma.it/museo
civiltaroma
📫 Off map at 28C1
✉ Piazza Gianni
Agnelli 10, EUR
☎ 06 592 6041
🕐 Tue–Sat 9–6.15,
Sun, hol 9–1.30
🚇 Magliana
🚌 714, 715 to Piazza
G. Marconi
💶 Expensive
🔁 Museo dell'Alto
Medioevo, Museo
Nazionale delle
Arti e Tradizioni
Popolari

The models and reconstructions inside this grandly fascist building give a sense of what life was really like in ancient

Rome and help put into context the fragments and artefacts that are the treasures of so many of the city's museums. There are busts and statues of the key figures of the day, reproductions of Roman furniture, surgical tools, musical instruments and sundials. The highlight is a giant scale model of Rome in the 4th century AD, at the time of Constantine, showing every building within the circular Aurelian walls.

Models recreate early Roman life

MUSEO DI ROMA IN TRASTEVERE ✪

www.comune.roma.it/museo
diroma.trastevere
📫 28B2
✉ Piazza Sant'Egidio 1/b
☎ 06 581 6563
🕐 Tue–Sun 10–8
🚌 23, 280 to Lungotevere
Sanzio
💶 Inexpensive

The museum opened in 1978 in a former Carmelite convent behind the church of Santa Maria in Trastevere. Everyday life in 17th- and 18th-century Italy, including festivals and customs, is illustrated by paintings, prints, reconstructions and waxworks, all among an interesting diversity of objects from the period when the popes ruled Rome. Memorabilia relating to famous Roman poets include Giuseppe Gioacchino Belli and Carlo Alberto Salustri (better known as Trilussa). Each of these local-dialect poets has a Trastevere square named after him.

MUSEO CIVICO DI ZOOLOGIA ✪

www.comune.roma.it/
museozoologia
📫 29D5
✉ Via Ulisse Aldrovandi 18
☎ 06 6710 9270
🕐 Tue–Sun 9–5
🚌 52, 53, 910 to zoo in Villa
Borghese
💶 Moderate

This museum, located alongside the city zoo or Bioparco (▶ 111), comprises the newly arranged civic zoological collection, following all the modern display criteria, and offers an important animal and insect collection. Among the most notable are the extinct species and the display of shells. An interesting diversion from the zoo itself and invaluable especially on a wet day.

MUSEO NAZIONALE DELLE PASTE ALIMENTARI ✪

This well-organised museum will tell you everything you ever needed to know about pasta (and a lot more besides). A portable CD player provides commentary (in Italian, English, Japanese, French or German) to the displays. The entire gamut of pasta production is covered, and there are examples of equipment and machinery used over the years, some rather questionable artworks on the pasta theme and photos of Italian and international personalities tucking into steaming plates of the nation's favourite dish.

MUSEO NAZIONALE ROMANO ✪✪

The museum is housed in two beautifully restored palaces, the **Palazzo Altemps**, a short distance from Piazza Navona, and the **Palazzo Massimo alle Terme**, near the station. The Altemps, one of Rome's finest Renaissance buildings, is a top-class assemblage of classical sculpture, mainly comprising the famous Cardinal Ludovico Ludovisi's collection, amassed in the 17th century. Note the beautiful 5th-century carved marble "Ludovisi Throne" dedicated to Athena. Also housed here is the Egyptian collection of antiques and portraits. The beautiful baroque frescoes in the rooms make a wonderful backdrop for the sculpture.

The upper floors of the Palazzo Massimo are bursting with archaeological goodies from the Roman Age (2nd century BC to 4th century AD) such as the exquisite mosaics from Livia's palace and a superb marble statue of a discus thrower (a Roman copy of a 5th-century BC Greek bronze). It is worth investing in the well-illustrated guidebook to negotiate your route around the extensive displays. Spacious and airy rooms open onto a courtyard, the exhibits are clearly labelled and each room has information sheets in English and Italian.

www.pastainmuseum.com
🕂 76B1
⊠ Piazza Scanderberg 117
☎ 06 699 1119
🕐 9.30–5.30
🚌 52, 53, 61, 62, 63, 71, 80, 160, 850 to Piazza San Silvestro
💶 Expensive

www.archeormiarti.benicult
ural.it

Palazzo Massimo alle Terme
🕂 29D4
⊠ Largo di Villa Peretti 1
☎ 06 3996 7700
🕐 Tue–Sun 9–7.45
🚇 Termini
🚌 64 and all services to Termini
♿ Good 💶 Moderate

Palazzo Altemps
🕂 29B3
⊠ Sant' Apollinare 44
☎ 06 683 3759
🕐 Tue–Sun 9–7.45
🚌 30, 70, 81, 116 to Corso
♿ Good 💶 Moderate

The Museo Nazionale Romano's vast cloister

Food & Drink

Italian cuisine is among the best (and, according to research, the most healthy) in the world. Each region has its own particular specialities, making use of the abundant raw ingredients that grow there, and some typically Roman dishes also owe much to the history of the city and its occupants.

Pasta

Classic Roman pasta dishes are *spaghetti alla carbonara* with bacon, eggs and *pecorino* (matured sheep's milk cheese, often used as an alternative to parmesan); *pasta all'arrabbiata* ('angry pasta' means hot) with tomatoes and fiery hot *peperoncino* (chilli); and *all'Amatriciana*, which is more or less the same with added bacon. *Pasta e ceci* is like a thick soup made with small pasta and chick peas, while *gnocchi* are hunger-busting potato dumplings served with butter and sage or tomato sauce.

Above: *Speciality pasta in many shapes and colours*

Below: *Making pizza*

Meat and Offal

Tradition has it that, while most of the butchered animal went to the rich, poor Romans had to make do with the left-over offal. This has led to an abundance of dishes using tripe, liver, kidneys, heart, bone marrow (*ossobuco* is a bone out of which the marrow is scooped) and brains. Perhaps the most extreme of these is *pagliata*, which is the intestine of a milk-fed calf, often served with *bucatini*, the thin, tube-like pasta it resembles. The best place for eating offal is in Testaccio where restaurants around the ex-abattoir Mattatoio have a long tradition of this type of cuisine.

Nowadays, however, even the most basic *trattoria* will offer beef and veal steaks, sausages (often with brown lentils) and flavoursome lamb from nearby Abruzzo. *Saltimbocca alla Romana* ('jumps into the mouth') is veal wrapped in raw ham and cooked with sage.

Fish

Apart from the traditional *baccalà* (cod fillets fried in batter and served as a snack or first course in *pizzerie*), the range of fish in Rome is immense and includes seafood such as mussels, clams (especially in *spaghetti alle vongole*), squid and prawns.

Vegetables and Snack Foods

Some of the vegetables common in Rome make good snacks—courgette (zucchini) flowers fried in batter, artichokes either steamed or baked, potato or spinach croquettes. *Supplì*, rice croquettes with a melted mozzarella filling, are another between-meals filler.

Other vegetables include *fave* (broad beans), often eaten with *pecorino* cheese in spring, spinach, broccoli, rocket and *puntarelle*, a crispy salad vegetable served in a vinegary sauce with anchovies.

Wines and Drinks

In Rome most of the house white wines come from Frascati and the Castelli Romani that surround the city. Orvieto in Umbria is another source of inexpensive white wine. House reds come from slightly further afield, Montepulciano from Abruzzo (not to be confused with the Vino Nobile of Montepulciano in Tuscany, which is a top-quality wine) and Chianti from Tuscany.

As well as wine, Italy has a massive range of drinks to stimulate the appetite before you eat or to help you digest the meal afterwards. *Aperitivi* include Campari and Martini-type aromatics, *prosecco*, a light fizzy white wine and *analcolici*, non-alcoholic versions of Campari and Martini. *Digestivi* include grappas that range from firewater to the smoothest of the smooth and *amari*, those thick, sticky concoctions made with herbs.

Fresh fish on sale at Campo de' Fiori

Dolci

If you don't opt for the ubiquitous *tiramisu*, for which nearly every restaurant has its own subtly different recipe, you could finish your meal with a slice of cake (*torta*); chocolate, fruit or *torta della nonna* with custard and pine kernels. Especially in winter, you'll be offered *crème caramel*, *crème brulée*, *panna cotta* ('cooked cream', a thick but light custard often served with berries), or ice-cream.

Frascati and Orvieto, two local sources for house white wines

28C2

✉ Through the Forum or Via di San Gregorio

☎ 06 3996 7700

🕐 9–1 hour before sunset

Ⓜ Colosseo

🚌 60, 75, 85, 87, 117, 175, 810 to Via di San Gregorio

PALATINO

Attached to the Forum (admission includes both), this is a peaceful, lush, hilly area covered with the remains of the massive palaces that the Roman emperors built for themselves. Most of what is on view dates from the 1st century AD. It can be frustrating to visit because many of the main attractions close at short notice and little is labelled, but there are guaranteed views of the Forum

(➤ 22) from the delightful semi-formal Orti Farnesiani (Farnese Gardens), laid out for Cardinal Alessandro Farnese in the 16th century. Underneath the gardens is a long tunnel built by Nero and decorated with stucco reliefs, some of which have survived. He may have intended this as a promenade for hot weather although some researchers believe that it led all the way to his massive palace overlooking the spot where the Colosseum stands today. Other highlights of the Palatine (although not always accessible) include the baths of Septimus Severus, the wall paintings in the house of Livia, traces of an 8th century BC village of huts and the complicated ground floor layouts of the Domus Flavia and the Domus Augustana.

💷 Expensive; tickets also valid for Colosseo

PALAZZO BARBERINI (➤ 19, TOP TEN)

PALAZZO COLONNA

www.galleriacolonna.it

✚ 28C3

✉ Via della Pilotta 17

☎ 06 678 4350

🕐 Sep–end Jul Sat 9–1

🚌 44, 46, 84, 715, 716, 780, 781, 810, 916 to Piazza Venezia

💷 Expensive

Some of the most beautiful ceiling frescoes in Rome adorn the opulent 18th-century galleries. There are some fine portraits in the first room but the eye automatically wanders through to the lavishly gilded Great Hall with its magnificent ceiling painting representing the life of Marcantonio Colonna. As you step down take care not to trip over the cannonball which became lodged there during the siege of Rome in 1849. Two ornate cabinets—one with inlaid carved ivory panels reproducing works by Raphael and Michelangelo (the central panel is his *Last Judgement* from the Sistine Chapel)—give the Room of the Desks its name. The Apotheosis of the Colonna Pope Martin V decorates the ceiling of the fourth room where Annibale Caracci's delightful *Bean Eater* makes an amusing change from more serious subjects. In the Throne Room a chair is kept ready (turned to the wall) in case of a papal visit.

Above: *Ruins of Roman palaces cover the Palatine Hill*

PALAZZO CORSINI ✪✪

Once the residence of Queen Christina of Sweden (► 14), the palace houses part of the national art collection (the more important part is at Palazzo Barberini, (► 19). The galleries, decorated with arresting *trompe l'oeil* frescoes, are filled predominantly with paintings from the 16th and 17th centuries. In room 1 Van Dyck's superb *Madonna della Paglia* and Murillo's *Madonna and Child* stand out among many other paintings of the same subject; one by Girolamo Siciolante de Sermoneta is frightening in its awfulness with an over-rosy, muscular baby seeming to choke on its mother's milk. Do not miss the paintings of the Bologna school in room 7, among which Guido Reni's richly coloured and expressive *St. Jerome* and melancholy *Salome*, Giovanni Lanfranco's very beautiful *St. Peter Healing St. Agatha* and the haunting *Ecce Homo* by Guercino are highlights.

✚ 28B3
✉ Via della Lungara 10
☎ 06 6880 2323
🕐 Tue–Sat 8.30–1.30, Sun 8.30–7
🚌 23, 116, 280, 870 to Lungotevere della Farnesina
♿ Few
🍴 Moderate
↔ Villa Farnesina

Looking towards the Palatino from the Forum

www.doriapamphilj.it
🔲 28C3
✉ Piazza del Collegio
Romano 2
☎ 06 679 7323
🕐 Apartments guided tours
only 10.30–12.30. Gallery
10–5, closed Thu
🚌 62, 63, 81, 85, 95, 117,
119 and services to Via
del Corso; 44, 46, 84,
715, 716, 780, 781, 810,
916 to Piazza Venezia
💶 Expensive

PALAZZO DORIA PAMPHILJ

The seat of the noble Roman family since the late Renaissance, Palazzo Doria Pamphilj takes up an entire block of Via del Corso. Extensive renovations took place in 1996. In the grand reception rooms, through which you enter, and the original picture galleries with their elaborate frescoed ceilings, the paintings are hung exactly as they were in the 18th century, cluttered side by side from floor to ceiling. Four rooms now house masterpieces from the 15th to 17th centuries including works by Hans Memling, Raphael, Titian, Tintoretto and two early paintings by Caravaggio. The star of the collection is the Velasquez portrait of Doria Pope, Innocent X, resplendent in vermilion robes, majestically positioned in its own chamber. For an extra charge take a guided tour of the fascinating private apartments.

www.palazzoesposizioni.it
🔲 28C3
✉ Via Nazionale 194
☎ 06 488 5465
🕐 Temporarily closed for
restoration; for reopening
check tourist office
🚇 Repubblica, Cavour
🚌 H, 40, 60, 64, 70, 117,
170 to Via Nazionale

PALAZZO DELLE ESPOSIZIONI

Rome's purpose-built (1883) palace of the fine arts has had a chequered history. Apart from serving its original brief, the building has housed the Communist Party, been a mess for allied servicemen, a polling station and a public lavatory. After years of restoration it was relaunched in 1990, as a vibrant multi-media centre with a strong emphasis on film and video in addition to an active programme of Italian and international exhibitions (both historical and contemporary). The palazzo is undergoing further restoration and is due to open again to the public around early 2006.

🔲 28B3
✉ Piazza Madama
☎ 06 67061
🕐 First Sat in each month
10–6; guided visits in
Italian only
🚌 30, 70, 81, 87, 116, 492,
628 to Corso del
Rinascimento

PALAZZO MADAMA

This pretty little palace has been the seat of the Italian senate since 1871, hence the armed police and military guard. It was built as the Medici family's Roman residence in the 16th century although the Madame after whom it was named was Margaret of Parma, an illegitimate daughter of Emperor Charles V who lived here in the 1560s. The icing-like stucco façade of cherubs and fruit was added in the 17th century.

🔲 76A1
✉ Piazza di Montecitorio
☎ 06 67061
🕐 First Sun in each month
10–6; guided tours in
Italian only
🚌 62, 63 and all services to
Via del Corso

PALAZZO DI MONTECITORIO

Bernini did the original designs for this concave palace, although all that remains of his work are the clock-tower, the columns and the window sills. In 1871 it became the Chamber of Deputies and had doubled in size by 1918. In the sloping piazza in front of the palace there are often political demonstrations; a strong police presence keeps people at a respectful distance from the main entrance through which Italy's 630 parliamentarians enter and exit. The obelisk in the piazza was brought from Egypt by Augustus in 10BC to act as the pointer of a giant (but, due to subsidence, inaccurate) sundial in nearby Campo Marzio. It was re-erected here in 1787.

PALAZZO DEL QUIRINALE ★★

This large orange palace, with the picture-book round look-out tower to its left, is the official residence of the President of the Republic of Italy and is guarded by exotically uniformed *Granatieri* who have been specially selected for their height and good looks. It was built in the 1570s as a papal summer palace for the fresh air on the highest of Rome's seven hills. Opposite, the two massive men with somewhat under-sized horses are ancient Roman copies of a 5th-century BC Greek sculpture of Castor and Pollux, the two god-knights who came to Rome's rescue during an early battle. The palace is open to the public only on Sunday mornings, with the gardens open on 2 June, Italian Republic Day.

Dazzling Palazzo Doria Pamphilj

www.quirinale.it

✚ 28C3

✉ Piazza del Quirinale

☎ 06 46991

🕐 Sun only 8.30–12. Closed Jul, Aug and most hols

🚌 40, 60, 64, 70, to Via IV Novembre

♿ Moderate

Italian Navy band marching out of the Quirinale

Discover Borromini's clever trompe l'oeil perspective in the courtyard of Palazzo Spada

PALAZZO SPADA ⊙⊙

Built in 1540, the ornate palace was acquired by Cardinal Bernardino Spada in the 17th century. In addition to housing his collection in the Galleria Spada, the palace is the seat of the Italian Council of State and thus under prominent *Carabinieri* guard. Among the 17th- and 18th-century paintings are a jewel-like *Visitation* attributed to Andrea del Sarto and works by Guercino and Rubens. Cardinal Spada also collected Roman sculpture—the restored *Seated Philosopher* is a highlight.

The most delightful aspect of the palace is Borromini's ingenious *trompe l'oeil* perspective in the lower courtyard (ask the attendants or porter to let you in). A long colonnade stretches out to a large statue at the end. Go closer to see that the colonnade is in fact only a quarter of the length it seems, and the statue much smaller than it first appears.

🗺 28B3
✉ Piazza Capo di Ferro 13
☎ 06 686 1158
🕐 Tue–Sat 8.30–7.30, Sun 9–6.30
🚌 280 to Lungotevere dei Tebaldi; H, 8, 63, 680, 780 to Via Arenula
♿ Moderate

PALAZZO VENEZIA ⊙⊙

Rome's most important collection of medieval decorative arts includes fine examples of Byzantine jewellery, silver work, ceramics, porcelain, tapestries and armour. There is a superb group of intricately carved Florentine wooden marriage chests, some small 16th-century bronzes and fine religious paintings by early Renaissance artists. Palazzo Venezia often hosts special exhibitions in the opulent main halls overlooking the piazza. Mussolini used the impressive, vast Sala del Mappamondo as his office.

🗺 28C3
✉ Via del Plebiscito 118
☎ 06 6999 4318
🕐 Tue–Sun 8.30–7; times may vary
🚌 44, 46, 84, 715, 716, 780, 781, 810, 916 to Piazza Venezia
♿ Few ⓘ Moderate

PANTHEON (► 20, TOP TEN)

PASQUINO
Physically, Pasquino has seen better days; all that remain
of this 3rd-century BC sculpture near Piazza Navona, are a
twisted torso and a weather-beaten face. But, for several
centuries after he was propped up here in the early 16th
century Pasquino played an important role as Rome's most
talkative 'talking statue'. During the days of papal rule (until
1870) there were few safe outlets for dissent and those
with political or social axes to grind came at dead of night
to attach their written complaints to one of the talking
statues.

✚	28B3
✉	Piazza di Pasquino
🚌	46, 64 and services to Corso Vittorio Emanuele

PIAZZA BARBERINI
The traffic-filled square at the foot of Via Veneto, the street
that was the hub of the *Dolce Vita* days of swinging Rome
in the 1960s, contains two fountains designed by Bernini
in the 1640s for the Barberini family. At the join with Via

✚	28C4
✉	Piazza Barberini
Ⓜ	Barberini
🚌	61, 62, 175, 492 to Piazza Barberini

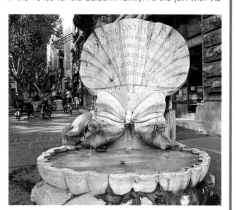

Bernini's Fontana della Api in Piazza Barberini

Veneto is the Fontana delle Api whose grotesquely large
bees (the Barberini family crest) crawl over the
unassuming basin. In the middle of the square is the far
more dramatic *Tritone*, whose well-muscled body is
supported by his own fish-tail legs and four dolphins as he
enthusiastically blows water through a vast sea-shell.

PIAZZA DEI CAVALIERI DI MALTA
Piranesi, famous for his surreal etchings of Roman views,
designed this peaceful piazza in 1765 and decorated it with
the symbols and devices of the Order of the Knights of
Malta whose priory is here. In the door of the priory is a
peep-hole which offers a magnificent miniature view of the
dome of St. Peter's seen beyond the tree-lined avenue of
the priory's garden. This part of the city, the Aventine, has
always been a genteel residential area.

✚	28C2
✉	Piazza dei Cavalieri di Malta
🚌	23, 30, 44, 95, 170, 280, 716, 781 to Lungotevere Aventino

The Historic Centre

Distance
4km (2.5 miles)

Time
2 hours without stops, 3½ hours with

Start point
Piazza Farnese
 28B3
to Corso Vittorio Emanuele

End point
Piazza del Popolo
28C4
Flaminio
to Piazzale Flaminio

Lunch
Hostaria Romanesca (€)
✉ Campo de' Fiori 40
☎ 06 686 4024
⊘ Closed Monday

Combine this walk with visits to the Forum and the Vatican and you can claim to have 'done' Rome.

From Piazza Farnese take Vicolo dei Baulari into Campo de' Fiori (➤ 37), where you can have an early lunch. Go to the far left-hand corner and into Piazza della Cancelleria.

Palazzo della Cancelleria (now Vatican offices) was built in 1485–1513 for a great-nephew of the Pope.

Turn right on Corso Vittorio Emanuele; cross at the lights. Continue down Via Cuccagna into Piazza Navona. Halfway up the piazza, Corso Agone leads to Palazzo Madama; Via Salvatore runs alongside, to San Luigi dei Francesi on the left. Continue to the Pantheon.

Pause, watch the activity, or have an expensive coffee.

Take the right-hand alley opposite the Pantheon, Vicolo della Maddalena, turn right down Via del Vicario into Piazza del Montecitorio. Follow Via di Guglia, in front of the palazzo, turn left at Via dei Pastini into Piazza di Pietra.

Here there are columns of a 2nd-century AD temple of Hadrian.

Walk past the columns, down Via di Pietra, cross Via del Corso and continue straight up Via di Muratte to the Trevi fountain. Follow Via della Stamperia, right of the fountain, turn right up Via del Tritone, cross and turn left on Via Due Macelli to Piazza di Spagna.

Rest by Bernini's Fontana della Barcaccis to observe the vitality as tourists and shoppers converge.

Climb the Spanish Steps, turn left, past Villa Medici (16th century, now the French Academy), take the path on the right to the Pincio Gardens.

Here are wonderful views over Piazza del Popolo.

PIAZZA FARNESE ✪✪

Dominated by Palazzo Farnese, which was designed for Farnese Pope Paulo III in the 1530s by—among others—Michelangelo, this spacious, nearly traffic-free square is a peaceful contrast to the nearby buzz of Campo de' Fiori (➤ 37) and a good spot for a quiet rest. The palace is now the French Embassy and at night Caracci's ceiling paintings on the first floor are illuminated. The two vast granite fountains were assembled in the 17th century from bath-tubs found at Caracalla's baths (➤ 75). They are decorated with lilies, the Farnese family crest.

☩ 28B3
✉ Piazza Farnese
🚌 46, 62, 64 and services to Corso Vittorio Emanuele

PIAZZA NAVONA (➤ 21, TOP TEN)

PIAZZA DEL POPOLO ✪✪✪

For the Grand Tourists of the 18th and 19th centuries this was the first sight of Rome as their luggage-laden carriages trundled through the Porta del Popolo. It was also where condemned criminals were executed (by having their heads smashed with hammers until the more humane guillotine took over in the early 19th century). It is overlooked to the east by the Pincio Gardens, which has marvellous views over the historic city centre and to the Vatican. The two apparently identical churches at the end of Via del Corso were built in the late 17th century by Rainaldi; looks can deceive though and, to fit into the available space, one of them actually has an oval rather than a round dome. Domenico Fontana designed the fountain (1589) around the 3,000-year-old obelisk that Emperor Augustus brought from Egypt.

☩ 28C4
✉ Piazza del Popolo
🚇 Flaminio
🚌 117, 119, 628, 926 to Piazza del Popolo

Looking down the Via del Corso from Piazza del Popolo

PIAZZA DELLA REPUBBLICA ✪

A rather seedy square whose once elegant colonnade is now occupied by adult cinemas and tourist-trapping bars, one side is dominated by the 3rd-century AD remains of the baths of Diocletian, into which Michelangelo incorporated the church of Santa Maria degli Angeli in 1563. The enticingly voluptuous nymphs (1901) of Mario Rutelli's *Fontana delle Naiadi* were greeted with scandalised horror when they were unveiled in 1910, but they have aged badly and their bodies are pock-marked by pollution.

☩ 29D3
✉ Piazza della Repubblica
🚇 Repubblica
🚌 40, 64, 84, 86, 90, 170, 175, 492, 910, H to Piazza della Repubblica

59

28C4
Piazza di Spagna
Spagna
119 to Piazza di Spagna

The perennially popular Spanish Steps afford a bird's-eye view across the city

PIAZZA DI SPAGNA ★★★

The sweeping Spanish Steps, designed in 1720 to connect the piazza with the French church of Trinità dei Monti, are now usually smothered with tourists, Italian soldiers and street-vendors who compete for space with tubs of magnolias in springtime and a life-size nativity scene at Christmas. The piazza gets its name from the Spanish Embassy which was here in the 17th century, and has been a compulsory stop for visitors to Rome since the 18th and 19th centuries when local tradesmen, models, unemployed servants and beggars mingled hopefully with the foreign artists, writers and Grand Tourists who congregated here. Keats lived and died in an apartment here (▶ 45). The low-lying Fontana della Barcaccia (fountain of the broken boat) at the bottom of the steps was designed by Pietro Bernini, father of the more famous Gian Lorenzo, in 1627 for Barberini Pope Urban VIII; the bees and suns were taken from the Barberini family crest. To the southeast, in Piazza Mignanelli, is a statue of the Virgin Mary on top of a column. This was erected in 1857 when Pope Pius IX proclaimed the doctrine of the Immaculate Conception, holding that the Virgin was the only person ever to have been born without original sin.

Attractive Ponte Sant'Angelo incorporates arches of Emperor Hadrian's original bridge, the Pons Aelius

PIRAMIDE CESTIA ✪

An engineer could tell you that this is nothing like as well-built as the Egyptian originals that inspired magistrate Caius Cestis (in Italian, *Caio Cestio*) when he was designing his own tomb in the 1st century BC—a time when the fashion for all things Egyptian was at its height. For all that, this 27-m (89-ft) high pyramid has stood the test of time and makes a somewhat surreal landmark next to the Porta San Paolo, one of the original gateways into Rome.

➕ 28C1
✉ Piazzale Ostiense
Ⓜ Piramide
🚌 3, 60, 75, 118, 715 to Piramide
↔ Protestant Cemetery

PONTE SANT'ANGELO ✪✪

Certainly the most elegant of the bridges over the Tiber, Bernini designed the ten angels which adorn its balustrades, each displaying one of the devices of Christ's passion, in 1667. Their ecstatically swooning expressions earned them the nickname of the 'Breezy Maniacs'. (Two more angels, deemed too beautiful to withstand the rigours of the Roman climate, are on show in the church of Sant'Andrea delle Fratte in Via di Sant'Andrea delle Fratte.) Most of the bridge dates from the 17th and 19th centuries but the central arches are the remains of the bridge that Emperor Hadrian built here in the 1st century AD to lead to his tomb (now Castel Sant'Angelo, 17).

➕ 28B3
✉ Ponte Sant'Angelo
🚌 40, 62 to Lungotevere Castello; 30, 34, 49, 87, 926, 990 and services to Piazza Cavour

Via Appia Antica (The Appian Way)

Distance
9km/5.5 miles (3km/2 miles to
tomb of Cecilia Metella)

Time
Whole walk with minimum of
stops 3 hours; to tomb of
Cecilia Metella 1 hour without
stops, 2–3 hours with stops

Start point
Porta di San Sebastiano
 29D1
118

End point
Via Appia Nuova
 29E1
663, 664, 765

Lunch
Cecilia Metella (▶ 93);
closed Mon. Beyond this
there are no bars or
restaurants so take your own
refreshments.

Via Appia Antica was
built in 312 BC by Appius
Claudius Caecus

This is a long walk and you may decide to finish at the
tomb of Cecilia Metella, about 3km (2 miles) from the start
point. Try to go on a Sunday, when the Via Appia is closed
to traffic apart from buses and wedding parties.

Go straight through Porta San Sebastiano
(▶ 63) and follow the road to the entrance to
the Catacombs of San Callisto (▶ 37).

On the left is the church of Domine Quo Vadis, which has
the imprints of Christ's feet, left when he appeared to St.
Peter who was trying to escape from Rome.

Bear right down Via Ardeatina, past the
Catacombs of Domitilla to the Fosse Ardeatine.

This is now a moving memorial to the 335 Italians who
were shot here by Nazis during World War II.

Follow Vicolo delle Sette Chiese back to the Via
Appia and turn right at the Basilica San
Sebastiano.

Opposite is the 4th-century tomb of Romulus (son of
Emperor Maxentius) and the remains of Maxentius's
stadium. Beyond this is the round tomb of Cecilia Metella,
wife of a rich 1st-century BC Roman. Stop for lunch here or
finish your walk.

From now on the traffic eases as the road, paved with
its original vast, uneven cobblestones, cuts straight across
the country. The cobbles are of Latium whitish lava stone.
The route here is lined by the attractively crumbling tombs
of ancient Romans. Along the stretch up to Via Erode
Attico there are several modern villas, but beyond that the
view gives way to farmland.

The walk finishes at the junction with Via del
Casal Rotondo, where another massive round
tomb has been converted into a farmhouse.

About half-way along this stretch are the remains of
aqueducts and the complex of buildings (including a
nyphaeum near the roadside) that made up the 2nd-
century AD Villa of the Quintilli.

Turn left at Via del Casal Rotondo and walk
until you reach Via Appia Nuova where you can
take a bus back into the centre.

PORTA SAN SEBASTIANO ❂

The best-preserved of Rome's ancient gateways, the Porta San Sebastiano, leading to the Via Appia Antica (▶ 62), was rebuilt in the 5th century AD. Today it houses a rather dry museum on the history of the Roman city walls, the highlight of which is a stretch of walkway along the top of the 3rd century AD Aurelian wall.

➕ 29D1
✉ Via di Porta San Sebastiano 18
☎ 06 7047 5284
🕐 Tue–Sat 9–7, Sun 9–2
🚌 218, 660 to Porta San Sebastiano
💷 Inexpensive

PROTESTANT CEMETERY ❂

In fact this serene spot is called the non-Catholic rather than the Cimitero Protestante (Protestant cemetery) but, in the first years after its establishment in 1738, most of its occupants were Protestant and the name has stuck. A map at the entrance will help you locate the final resting places of, among others, English poets Keats and Shelley, Julius, the son of German poet J. W. von Goethe, and Antonio Gramsci, the founder of the Italian Communist Party.

➕ 28C1
✉ Via Caio Cestio 6
🕐 Tue–Sat 9–5, Sun 9–2, but subject to change without notice
🚌 3, 23, 60, 75, 118, 280 to Via Marmorata or Piazza di Porta San Paolo
💷 Donation

SANT'AGOSTINO ❂❂

An important early Renaissance Roman church containing a sculpture of the pregnant Mary by Sansovino (1518–21), an altar with Bernini angels and a Byzantine Madonna. The main attractions are, however, the paintings by Raphael and Guercino and Caravaggio's beautiful *Madonna di Loreto* (painted in 1606, just before he had to flee Rome to escape a murder charge). Caravaggio's realistic portayal of biblical figures as poor people, usually (as here) illuminated in the foreground and forming a strong diagonal across the picture, were criticised for lack of decorum because of their dirty feet, ripped clothes and perhaps too-human Madonna.

➕ 28C3
✉ Piazza S. Agostino
☎ 06 880 1962
🕐 8.30–12. 4–6.30
🚌 30, 70, 81, 87, 116 to Corso del Rinascimento

Did you know ?

Sant'Agostino was where many of Rome's most sought-after courtesans came to worship, attracting a large following of male admirers. For an attractive, go-getting Renaissance girl, life as the kept woman of a Roman aristocratic (or even a senior church man; many of the popes' so-called nephews were really their sons) could lead to riches and a successful career (like the mother of Lucrezia and Cesare Borgia who bought and ran three hotels).

SANT'ANDREA AL QUIRINALE ❂❂

A theatrical Bernini gem (1628–70) decorated in pink marble. The portico beckons and the interior embraces soothingly. The oval space (imposed by site restrictions), the short distance between entrance and altar, the gold ceiling, dark chapels and four massive richly veined columns all combine to pull one's gaze to the altar and Cortese's marble-framed *Martyrdom* borne by angels. On the pediment above, St. Andrew soars to heaven, while garlanded *putti* perch and fishermen recline. The architectural expression of Bernini's sculptural ideals, it was his personal favourite, built for no payment. Also worth noting are the walnut-lined sacristy and chapels of St. Stanislao (paintings by Sebastiano del Pozzo, statues by Legros).

➕ 29D3
✉ Via del Quirinale 29
☎ 06 474 4872
🕐 Wed–Mon 8–12, 4–7
🚌 71, 1176 to Via Milano; 70, 117, 170 to Via Nazionale

28C3
Corso Vittorio Emmanuele
06 686 1339
7.30–12.30, 4.30–7.30
46, 64 and services to Corso Vittorio Emmanuele; 30, 70, 81, 87, 116, 492, 628 to Corso del Rinascimento

SANT'ANDREA DELLA VALLE ✪

Another great Counter-Reformatory church to put Protestantism on the defensive and accommodate yet another new Order (the Theatines, founded in 1524). Designed by Della Porta (1591), it has a superb and imposing travertine façade (Rainaldi, 1655–63) and Carlo Maderno's impressive dome (1622), which is second only to that of St. Peter's and also contains one of the church's important baroque fresco cycles. Other frescoes, by competitors Lanfranco and Domenichino in the dome, and Domenichino's *Scenes from the Life and Death of St Andrew* in the apse, have been restored. Opera fans note that this is where the opening scene of Puccini's *Tosca* takes place.

29D3
Via del Quirinale 23 (corner of Via Quattro Fontane)
06 488 3261
Mon–Fri 10–1, 3–5.30, Sun 12–1, 3–5.30
Repubblica, Barberini
40, 60, 64, 70, 117, 170 to Via Nazionale

Borromini made the most of a restricted space when he designed the church of San Carlo alle Quattro Fontane

SAN CARLO ALLE QUATTRO FONTANE ✪✪

This was Borromini's first major work (1638) after a long apprenticeship under Maderno. It is difficult for modern eyes to appreciate the revolutionary quality of this tortured man's work. He overturned the Renaissance assumptions that architecture was based on the proportions of the human body, designing it instead around geometric units. The manipulation of the minuscule space is certainly ingenious, not least in the swiftly shrinking coffers of the honeycombed dome, which give an illusion of size. The changing rhythms inside are also present on the façade, Borromini's last work (1667). The three bays of the lower half read concave-convex-concave while those above are all concave.

28C2
Piazza Santa Cecilia in Trastevere 22
06 589 9289
10–12, 4–6. Cavallini frescoes, Tue and Thu 10–12, Sun 11.15–12.15
56, 60, 75, 710, 780 to Viale Trastevere
Donation expected for Cavallini frescoes and excavations

SANTA CECILIA IN TRASTEVERE ✪✪

Approached through a delightful courtyard, this church contains one of the most beautiful baroque sculptures in Rome (Stefano Maderno, 1599), showing a tiny Saint Cecilia, the patron saint of music. Supposedly in the position of her nasty death (it took her three days to die), her head poignantly turns from our gaze. There are also the great Cavallini's frescoes of the *Last Judgement* (1293), painted in beautifully soft powdery blues, greens and pinks of the trumpeting angels' wings. Underneath the church, the remains of a Roman house and shops, including a mosaic, can still be seen.

SAN CLEMENTE (► 23 TOP TEN)

[handwritten: SE I floor a statin]

SANTA CROCE IN GERUSALEMME ✪

This church bursts with relics; indeed it was built (1144) for that very purpose. In the Chapel of the Relics are pieces of the True Cross and thorns from Christ's Crown brought to Rome by the Empress Helena in 320, whose crypt is built on soil from Mount Golgotha. The chapel contains some wonderfully ornamental mosaics showing scenes decked with flowers and birds.

✚ 29E2
✉ Piazza di Santa Croce in Gerusalemme
☎ 06 701 4769
🕐 7–7
🚌 117, 186, 218, 650, 850 to Piazza Santa Croce in Gerusalemme 12

SAN FRANCESCO A RIPA ✪

A 13th-century monastery was built on the site of an inn where St. Francis of Assisi supposedly stayed but the present church is baroque (1692, by de' Rossi, working under Bernini). Architecturally uninteresting, it does however house one of Bernini's most splendid works (*The Blessed Ludovica Albertoni*, 1674). Framed in the last left chapel, she is best approached head-on from the nave. Depicted in feverish death throes after her life of good works, the agonized writhings of the deeply cut white folds of her clothes create a powerful impact. The textures of hair, skin or the bed are not differentiated and the whiteness is intensified by the dark foreground drapes, close enough to touch.

✚ 28B2
✉ Piazza San Francesco d'Assisi
☎ 06 588 1331
🕐 7–12, 4–7
🚌 23, 280, 630, 780 to Largo di Torre Argentina then tram 8 to Viale Trastevere

SAN GIOVANNI IN LATERANO ✪✪✪

This was the home of the papacy from Constantine until 1305, and is the present cathedral of Rome. In short, it is an important place. The early buildings suffered from fire and neglect after the Pope's exile to Avignon and the subsequent move to the Vatican, and the present-day San Giovanni dates from the baroque: including Fontana's palace and portico (1585), Gallei's façade and Borromini's nave (1650), which incorporates the columns of the original basilica inside a new and vigorous structure, creating niches for figures of the Apostles. Look out for the 5th-century mosaics in the baptistery apse and the bronze door (1190) of the chapel of St. John the Evangelist. The baptistery was damaged by a bomb in 1993.

✚ 29E2
✉ Piazza di San Giovanni in Laterano
☎ 06 6988 6433
🕐 Cloisters 9–7, baptistery 8–12.30, 3.30–7; can vary check first
🚇 San Giovanni
🚌 3, 6, 81, 85, 87, 117, 850 to Piazza di San Giovanni in Laterano

Borromini's nave within Rome's cathedral church

Andrea Pozzo's beautiful and fantastic trompe l'oeil ceiling in Sant'Ignazio di Loyola depicts the saint's entry into Paradise

---

🕀 29D2
✉ Piazza di San Gregorio Magno
☎ 06 700 9357
🕐 9–12, 3–6
🚇 Circo Massimo
🚌 81, 117, 118, 628, 673 to Via di San Gregorio

SAN GREGORIO MAGNO ✪

Originally Gregory the Great's monastery (575), from where he set out to take Christianity to England, it is now a feast of baroque, with Soria's masterpiece of a façade (1629) sitting decorously at the top of a splendid flight of stairs. More interesting than the church interior is the adjacent Oratory. The first room contains the table (supported by 3rd-century carved griffins) from which Gregory was said to have fed 12 poor people daily. In the central chapel (dedicated to St.Andrew) is the lovely misty-coloured fresco by Reni of *St. Andrew Adoring the Cross* and Domenichino's even lovelier *Scourging*.

🕀 29D3
✉ Piazza di Sant'Ignazio
☎ 06 679 4406
🕐 7.30–12.30, 3–7
🚌 62, 81, 492, 628 to Via del Corso; 116 to Largo di Torre Argentina

SANT'IGNAZIO DI LOYOLA ✪

The interior of this second Jesuit church (Il Gesù, ➤ 43) is a late-baroque (1626–50) assault on the senses, epitomised by Jesuit artist, Andrea Pozzo's astonishing fresco in the nave—*Apotheosis of St. Ignatius* (1691). An extraordinary feat of perspective, the *trompe l'oeil* architecture becomes indistinguishable from the real. The dome, too, is painted (find the spot, move and watch the perspective distort). Similarly sumptuous are St. Aloysius' tomb with its lapis lazuli urn and the altar with Legros' relief sculpture (right transept 1698–9). The friezes are by one of the baroque period's finest, Algardi.

🕀 28C3
✉ Corso Rinascimento, 40
☎ 06 686 4987
🕐 Mon–Fri 8.30–5, Sat, Sun 9–12
🚌 30, 70, 81, 87, 116, 492, 628 and services to Corso del Rinascimento

SANT'IVO ALLA SAPIENZA ✪

Not far from the Pantheon in Piazza Sant'Eustachio is the domed church of Sant'Ivo alla Sapienza, one of Borromini's masterpieces. Built in the grounds of the Palazzo alla Sapienza, the University of Rome until 1935, the church is worth visiting for its extraordinary spiralling dome surmounted by a crown of flames. Entrance to the church is through the cloister.

A Walk from the Celian Hill

The green and peaceful Celian hill overlooks the Colosseum, and adjoins the Baths of Caracalla and the Circo Massimo.

Starting at San Gregorio Magno (➤ 66), turn right up Via di San Gregorio and take the first right, Clivo di Scauro which runs under the flying buttresses that support Santi Giovanni e Paolo (➤ 33), opposite are the studios of Canale 5 (one of Berlusconi's TV stations). Continue straight up Via di San Paolo della Croce, under the 1st-century AD Arch of Dolabella and past the gateway of San Tommaso in Formis.

San Tommaso in Formis has a 13th-century mosaic of Christ freeing a black and a white slave. To the left is the church of San Stefano Rotondo (➤ 74), and on the right is Santa Maria in Domnica (➤ 69); the fountain was erected in 1931 using a 16th-century sculpture of a boat. Next to the church is the entrance to Villa Celimontana park.

At the bottom of Via della Navicella bear right down Via Druso and turn right along Viale delle Terme di Caracalla, passing the baths (➤ 75) to reach Circo Massimo (➤ 39).

Rest on the grass and let your imagination drift back to the chariot races.

Turn left on Viale Aventino and take the first right up Via di Circo Massimo. Follow this to Piazzale Ugo La Malfa and take the second left, Via di Valle Murcia following it up to the top .

Here there is a small orange garden with views over Rome. Following Via di Santa Sabina you reach Santa Sabina (➤ 73) and Santi Bonifacio e Alessio with its 18th-century façade, cosmati doorway and belltower.

Continue straight to Piazza dei Cavalieri di Malta (➤ 57). Turning left just before the piazza down Via di Porta Lavernale will take you back down to Via Marmorata for buses, but first have lunch near Piramide.

Distance
4km (2.5 miles)

Time
2 hours without stops,
3 hours with

Start point
San Gregorio Magno
🚇 29D2
🚇 Circo Massimo
🚌 To Circo Massimo Piazza di Colosseo

End point
Via Marmorata
🚇 29C2
🚇 Ostiense
🚌 to Via Marmorata

Lunch
Taverna Cestia (€€) (➤ 98).
✉ Viale Piramide Cestia 87
☎ 574 3754
🚫 Closed Mon
🚇 Piramide
🚌 3, 60, 75, 118, 715 to Piramide

+ 28C3
⊠ Piazza S Luigi dei Francesci 5
☎ 06 688271
🕐 8–12.30, 3.30–7 (closed Thu pm)
🚌 30, 70, 81, 87, 116, 492, 628 to Corso del Rinascimento

SAN LUIGI DEI FRANCESI ✪✪

Founded in 1518 by Cardinal Giulio de' Medici (later Pope Clement VII) this, the French national church, is worth visiting mainly for its paintings, including a *St. Cecilia* by Domenichino (1616) and Reni. The *pièces de résistance* are, however, the works by Caravaggio, *The Calling of St. Matthew* and *The Martyrdom of St. Matthew* (1599), in the Contarelli chapel. Both exemplify the artist's use of artificial lighting which casts the backgrounds into deep darkness, focuses attention on the story's essential elements and moulds the remarkably everyday figures who dominate the foreground. This everyday quality was perceived as irreverent and the most notorious example, *St. Matthew and the Angel* (1602), is above the altar (note the dirty feet).

+ 29D4
⊠ Via Vittorio Veneto 27
☎ 06 487 1185
🕐 Cemetery: 9–12, 3–6; church 7–12, 3.30–7
🚇 Barberini
🚌 52, 53, 95, 116, 119 to Via Veneto

SANTA MARIA DELLA CONCEZIONE ✪✪

If you feel like contemplating immortality then visit this little church (1631–8), a Barberini initiative for the Capuchin monks. The sombre theme is spelt out on the tombstone of a Barberini ('here lie dust, ashes and nothing'), but reaches a climax in the musty odour of the bone-lined crypt where dead monks' remains decorate the ceiling and walls. The church is know for Guido Reni's painting *St. Michael Tempting the Devil*, in which the Devil is reputedly a portrait of Pamphili Pope Innocent X.

+ 29D4
⊠ Piazza della Bocca della Verità 18
☎ 06 678 1419
🕐 9–1, 3–6
🚌 30, 44, 81, 950 to Piazza della Bocca della Verità

SANTA MARIA IN COSMEDIN ✪✪✪

The austere intimacy of this lovingly restored 12th-century basilica in the heart of ancient Rome houses beautiful cosmati works so characteristic of Roman churches of the period. The Cosmati (actually several families but grouped together because of the preponderance of the name Cosma) were builders and designers but are best remembered for their luscious decorations in marble and colourful mosaics. Examples can be seen here in the magnificent nave paving (1123), the raised choir, the paschal candlestick, the bishop's throne and, in particular, the beautiful *baldacchino* (1294). In the portico is the *Bocca della Verità* (mouth of truth)—legend has it that the mouth would bite the hand of he who lied—or more commonly she whose marital fidelity was questioned. In the sacristy are mosaics (706) from old St. Peter's.

Beautiful mosaics within the equally lovely medieval church of Santa Maria in Cosmedin

SANTA MARIA IN DOMNICA ✪✪

A haven of calm, this lovely church was rebuilt (817–24) in honour of the Virgin (who takes pride of place in the delightful apse mosaic showing saints striding through meadows). It is also known as *'La Navicella'* on account of the 16th-century copy of a Roman boat in front of the entrance. The boat is a fountain, made from an ancient stone galley; this may have been an offering made by a safely returned traveller. Pope Leo X added the portico and the ceiling. The theme of journeying continues in the 12 images of great delicacy and simplicity on the 11th-century wooden ceiling (among which are the ark, the tree of life and, in the middle, the Medici coat of arms). There is a notable 9th-century mosaic in the apse, which was commissioned by Pope Paschal I. Some excavated Roman remains are exhibited under the altar.

✚ 29D2
✉ Piazza della Navicella 10
☎ 06 700 1519
🕐 9–12, 3.30–6
Ⓜ Colosseo
🚌 81, 673 to Via della Navicella

SANTA MARIA SOPRA MINERVA ✪✪✪

Bernini's engaging obelisk-bearing baby elephant (1667) sits in the piazza in front of this typically eclectic church (built in 1280, completed in 1500, modified in the 17th century). Inside there is many a fine work: Bernini's wind-blown richly coloured marble monument to Maria Raggi (1643) and another to G. B. Vigevano (1617); Michelangelo's *Redeemer with his Cross* (1520); and the rich and lavish Aldobrandini chapel (della Porta and C. Maderna, 1600–5) once again bearing witness to important Roman families making their own mark on baroque Rome. The treats, however, are Renaissance, notably the stunning frescoes by Lippi. Saint Valentine was made the patron saint of lovers here in 1465.

✚ 28C3
✉ Piazza della Minerva
☎ 06 679 3926
🕐 8–7
🚌 30, 40, 46, 62, 64, 70, 81, 87 and services to Largo di Torre Argentina

Bernini's highly unusual elephant statue in the middle of Piazza della Minerva

28C4

Piazza del Popolo 12

7–12, 4–7, hols 8–2,
4.30–7.30

Flaminio

117, 119 to Piazzale
Flaminio

SANTA MARIA DEL POPOLO ✪✪✪

The church is bursting with masterpieces. Part of the façade and interior are by Bernini, whose *Habbakuk* and *Daniel* statues are cramped into small niches in the Renaissance Chigi chapel (Raphael, 1516) along with mosaics. An angel visits Habbakuk and Daniel is praying with arms outstretched. Caravaggio and Carracci, the two dominant forces of baroque painting, are together in the Cerasi chapel (left transept). Caravaggio's *Conversion of St. Paul*, so dramatically foreshortened that he seems to fall off the canvas, and the strong diagonals of the *Crucifixion of St. Peter* share the space with Carracci's *Assumption of the Virgin* (1601). Pinturicchio (c1485), whose work can be seen in the frescoes, is represented by paintings in the Della Rovere chapel.

The church is worth visiting for any one of these works; to have them all under one roof nestling against the Roman wall in this magnificent piazza is a treat indeed.

Below: *Santa Maria del Popolo's rich interior is crammed with works of art*

28B2

Piazza Santa Maria in
Trastevere

06 581 9443

8.30–12.30, 4–7.30

8, 630, 780, H to Viale
Trastevere

SANTA MARIA IN TRASTEVERE ✪✪✪

The 12th-century mosaics on the façade create a magical backdrop to the piazza, the heart and hub of this characteristic quarter, particularly when illuminated. Inside the basilica, is the glorious expanse of gold of the apse mosaic. This is the oldest church in Rome dedicated to Mary (3rd and 4th centuries, rebuilt in the 12th), and she is represented with almost equal stature to Christ in the mosaic's upper panel (c1140) below a fan-like kaleidoscopic design of luxuriant blue. In the panels below are a series of exquisitely delicate representations of her life (by Pietro Cavallini, working in the late 13th century). There is also a cosmati floor and a ceiling by Domenichino designed in 1617.

SANTA MARIA DELLA VITTORIA   ✪✪

You could be forgiven for leaving Santa Maria della Vittoria off a busy itinerary; its baroque façade and interior are not the best examples in Rome, despite having been worked on by the architects Maderno and Soria and containing paintings by Domenichino, Guercino and Reni. However, it

does contain Bernini's Cornaro Chapel and his *Ecstasy of St. Teresa*, one of the finest pieces of baroque sculpture, making the church well worth a detour. The restored *St. Teresa* embodies Bernini's ideas of capturing the dramatic moment, in this case the saint's religious ecstasy (erotic to modern perceptions) as the Cornaro cardinals watch down from the side chapel.

➕ 29D4
✉ Via XX Settembre 17
🕐 7.30–12, 3–6; but hours may vary
Ⓜ Repubblica

SAN PIETRO (ST PETER'S)
(► 26, TOP TEN)

SAN PIETRO IN MONTORIO   ✪✪

In the church is Bernini's Raimondi chapel, an important precursor to the Cornaro chapel (► Santa Maria della Vittoria, above) for its lighting effects. More significant is Bramante's *tempietto* ('little temple') in the courtyard of the adjoining monastery (1502), a seminal work in the history of architecture. Its perfectly proportioned simplicity and dignity, so in keeping with the commemoration of the (alleged) spot of Peter's crucifixion, expresses the Renaissance ideals of emulating classical architecture.

➕ 28B2
✉ Piazza San Pietro in Montorio
☎ 06 581 3940
🕐 9–12, 4–6
🚌 870 to Gianicolo

SAN PIETRO IN VINCOLI   ✪✪

To appreciate Michelangelo's *Moses* without jostling for position in front of the memorial to Julius II, make an early start. Flanked by Leah and Rachel (ironically representing contemplation), he remains remarkably impervious to the clicking cameras and rustling guidebooks, his gaze reaching out to some indeterminate spot across the nave, his hands sagaciously pulling back his abundant beard. Sculpted from a single piece of Carrara marble between 1513 and 1516, Moses is built on a large scale with enormous legs weighing him down and exquisitely moulded musculature; he is a massive expression of power and strength. Nearby, under the altar, lie St. Peter's chains.

➕ 29D3
✉ Piazza San Pietro in Vincoli 4
☎ 06 488 2865
🕐 7.30–12.30, 3.30–6 (7 in summer)
Ⓜ Cavour, Colosseo
🚌 75, 84 to Via Cavour

Tradition has it that Santa Pudenziana stands on the site where St. Peter once lived

29D3
Via di S. Prassede 9a
06 488 2456
7–12, 4–6.30
Termini
16, 71, 75, 84 to Via Cavour-Piazza dell'Esquilino

SANTA PRASSEDE ✪✪

Santa Prassede has mosaics unrivalled in medieval Rome. The figure of Christ dominates the vault, flanked by saints and Pope Paschal I (who built the church in 817–24), distinguished by his square halo of the living. The apse mosaics are rich in symbols: the phoenix (resurrection), the eagle, ox, angel and lion (the evangelists) and the four rivers of Eden (earthly paradise). The glimmering intricacy of mosaics can be enjoyed up close in the small, enchanting side Chapel of St. Zeno. Behind the altar the saint deposits martyrs' blood and relics down the well beneath the nave. Worth noting is a bust of Monsignor Giovanni Battista Santoni carved by Bernini when a teenager.

29D3
Via Urbana 160
06 481 4622
8–6
Termini, Cavour
74, 84 to Via Cavour-Piazza dell'Esquilino; 70, 71 to Via A de Pretis

SANTA PUDENZIANA ✪✪

The early Christian Basilica (401–17) was erected over ancient Roman baths and a house but tradition supposes this to be the site of the oldest church in Rome (AD145). It has seen many changes over the centuries; witness the baroque opulence of the Caetani chapel, through which you descend to reach the ancient remains; ask to see this. The main impact, comes from the stunning 4th-century apse mosaics set in the nave's serene context.

SANTI QUATTRO CORONATI ✪

Make sure you ask to visit the Oratory of St. Silvester with its delightful frescoes (1246), *Scenes from the Life of Constantine*, situated in the adjoining convent. In soothing faded colours, and proof of how persistent was the influence of Byzantine art in Rome, you can see poor, spotty Constantine being cured of the pox by Pope Silvester. On the ceiling is a unique cross of five majolica plates. The Chapel of Santa Barbara has remains of medieval frescoes, and there is a garden in the inner courtyard. The church of Santi Quattro Coronati (Four Crowned Saints) has a typically long and complicated history; originally 4th-century, it was rebuilt in the 12th, as you can see from the belltower and cosmati paving. It more resembles a castle than a church.

🗓 29D2
✉ Via dei Santi Quattro Coronati 20
☎ 06 7047 5427
🕐 Mon–Sat 9.30–12, 4.30–6, Sun 9.30–10.30, 4.30–6
🚌 3, 81, 85, 117, 218, 650, 850 to Via San Giovanni in Laterano

SANTA SABINA ✪✪

The light-bathed interior of this perfect, serene early Christian basilica was built for Peter of Illyria (422–32), the belltower and cloisters were added in 1218 when the church was given to St. Dominic and his newly formed order. Dominic's orange tree can be peeked at through a small gap in the portico. The church is named after the Roman Sabina martyred in Hadrian's time. Inside, the beautifully proportioned antique columns with their delicately carved Corinthian capitals support the nave arcading and 5th-century frieze. Unfortunately, the 5th-century mosaics on the apse and arch have not survived; the fresco reproductions are 15th-century.

🗓 28C2
✉ Piazza Pietro d'Illiria 1
☎ 06 57941
🕐 6.30–12.30, 4–7
🚌 3, 60, 73 75, 118, to Viale Aventino; 175 to Lungotevere Aventino

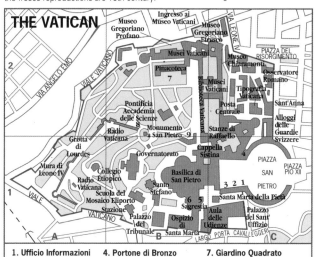

1. Ufficio Informazioni
2. Ufficio Postale
3. Arco delle Campane
4. Portone di Bronzo
5. Ufficio Scavi
6. Museo Storico Artistico
7. Giardino Quadrato
8. Fontana dell'Aquilone
9. Fontana del Sacramento

+ 29D2
✉ Via di Santa Stefano 7
☎ 06 481 9333
⏱ 9–1, 1.50–4.30 (times can vary so check first)
🚌 81, 673 to Via della Navicella

SANTO STEFANO ROTONDO ✪

Santo Stefano is one of the oldest round churches in Rome, c470, and has a contemplative ambience. Originally, the outer walls were further out, with circular and cross-shaped windows, and there were eight entrances. No evidence of an altar has been found (the present one is 13th-century); the two central columns supporting the lofty white-washed dome are also later additions. To the left of the present-day entrance a section of the original flooring has been painstakingly recreated using excavated marble fragments. Faded representations of gruesome martyrdoms (by Pomerancio and others c1600) adorn the walls.

SISTINE CHAPEL AND THE VATICAN MUSEUMS (▶ 24, TOP TEN)

+ 28C2
✉ Via del Teatro di Marcello
☎ 06 5752 50410
🚌 30, 44, 95, 170, 716, 781 to Via del Teatro di Marcello
❓ Tours available

TEATRO DI MARCELLO ✪✪✪

Here 2,000 years of Roman history can be seen at a glance. The lower part of the multi-levelled and many-styled building comprises the surviving two levels of a three-storey theatre that Julius Caesar started. Augustus finished the theatre in the 1st century BC and named it after one of his nephews. The elegant 16th-century palace, dramatically built on top of these crumbling remains (which served as, among other uses, a medieval fortress) and now divided into luxury apartments, was built by Baldassarre Peruzzi. The strange, reddish coloured protu-berance stuck on the southern end is a 1930s Fascist addition, supposedly in keeping with the style of the theatre. To the north are three delicate Corinthian columns, part of a Temple of Apollo which was rebuilt in the 1st century BC. In summer, classical music concerts are held outside the theatre (▶ 114).

Above: *the Temple of Vesta;*
Right: *Terme di Caracalla*

TEMPI DI VESTA E DELLA FORTUNA VIRILIS ✪✪

Neither of these photogenic, small but perfectly formed temples have anything to do with Vesta or *Fortuna Virilis* (manly fortune). The round one, which dates from the 1st century BC and is the same shape as the temple of Vesta in the Forum (➤ 22), was dedicated to Hercules. The rectangular one, dating from the 2nd century BC, was dedicated to Portunus, the god of harbours; this was the port area of ancient Rome. Across the piazza from the temples is the 4th-century double arch of Janus, named after the two-headed guardian of the underworld.

🚇 28C2
✉ Piazza della Bocca della Verità
🚌 81, 160, 628, 715 to Piazza della Bocca della Verità

TERME DI CARACALLA *Sq colosseum* ✪✪✪

Ancient Romans did not go to the baths just to keep clean but to relax, meet each other, discuss politics, exercise and even study. Even bathing itself was not merely a soak in a tub; the Romans started off with a sauna, followed by a scrape down, a hot bath, a tepid bath and, finally, a dive into the cold bath. The serene ruins of the baths that Caracalla built in the 3rd century AD include remains of each of these types of bath as well as gyms, a library and a complicated underfloor heating system. They are used for summer outdoor opera performances (➤ 114).

🚇 29D1
✉ Via delle Terme di Caracalla 52
☎ 06 3996 7700
🕐 Tue–Sun 9 to 1 hour before sunset, Mon 9–2
🚇 Circo Massimo
🚌 60, 75, 81, 175, 673 to Via delle Terme di Caracalla
♿ Few
💶 Moderate

➕ 28B1

✉ Area between Via
Marmorata and
Lungotevere Testaccio

🚌 3, 23, 30, 75, 280, 716 to
Via Marmorata; 95, 170,
781 to Lungotevere
Testaccio

*Exclusive shopping on
the Via Condotti*

TESTACCIO ✪

Although well-known to Romans, who flock to its traditional restaurants and less-traditional nightclubs in the
evenings, the Testaccio area is off the main tourist track.
Most of its buildings are tall, courtyarded residential
blocks, dating from the end of the 19th century and
designed to include schools, crèches and shops, but it is
the area around Monte Testaccio that sees the action,
especially at night and during the summer (➤ 114–15).
The *monte* is made up of millions of broken *amphorae*,
dumped here by ancient Roman dockers when this was
the port area where ships unloaded their cargo, including

the oil that was transported in these clay pots. Opposite the hill is the old *mattatoio*—the most sophisticated abattoir in Europe when it opened in 1891—now used for concerts, art exhibitions and other cultural events.

VIA CONDOTTI ✪

Usually packed with well-heeled fashion victims and tourists, this elegant street is the heart of designer Rome, and most of the big Italian names have shops here or on the adjoining streets (➤ 108). It runs from Via del Corso to Piazza di Spagna and has an excellent view of the Spanish Steps. Keats and Liszt visited Caffè Greco at number 86.

🞜 76B2
✉ Via Condotti
🅜 Spagna
🚌 117, 119 to Via Condotti

From high above, the designer delights of the Via Condotti are as yet unseen

Below: *the Sale delle Prospettive, and (inset) Raphael's fresco of Cupid, Villa Farnesina;*
Right: *view across rooftops to St. Peter's*

✚ 28B3
✉ Via della Lungara 230
☎ 06 6802 7268
🕐 Mon–Sat 9–1 and first Sun of month
🚌 23, 280 to Lungotevere della Farnesina
🎟 Moderate

VILLA FARNESINA ⭐⭐

Baldassare Peruzzi built this delicate little villa in 1508 for the rich banker Agostino Chigi, who was also a patron of Raphael. Now it is used for temporary exhibitions although its otherwise empty rooms are also worth visiting for their spectacular frescoes by Raphael, whose *Triumph of Galatea* is on the ground floor along with the *Loggia di Psiche* which he designed, and Sodoma, whose seductive fresco of the *Marriage of Alexander the Great and Roxanne* is painted against a *trompe l'oeil* background of views of contemporary Rome.

✚ 28C5
✉ Piazzale di Villa Giulia 9
☎ 06 322 6571
🕐 Tue–Sun 8.30–7.30
🚇 Flamino
🚌 3, 19 to Viale delle Belle Arti
♿ Few
🎟 Moderate
↔ Galleria Nazionale d'Arte Moderna e Contemporanea (➤ 42)

VILLA GIULIA ⭐⭐⭐

This charming palace with its shady courtyards houses the national collection of Etruscan art, although it was originally built in 1550–5 as a summer residence for Pope Julius III. The central loggia and *nymphaeum*, decorated with frescoes and mosaics, were frequently copied in later 16th-century Italian villas.

The Etruscans arrived in Italy towards the end of the 8th century BC and settled between the Arno and the Tiber, the area known as Etruria (present day Lazio, Umbria and southern Tuscany). The objects unearthed from Etruscan tombs in the region bear witness to the sophistication of the civilisation. The highlight of the collection is the 6th-century BC terracotta sarcophagus of a husband and wife reclining on a divan found at the necropolis of Cerveteri and known as the Sacrophagus of the Spouses. Have a look at some of the jewellery, and you will see that design has not necessarily changed all that much since.

Excursions from the City

Just as all roads lead to Rome, they also lead from it. To escape the chaos, crowds or summer heat dozens of destinations are within easy reach. Heading south are the fascinating excavations of Ostia Antica; further towards Naples are the sandy beaches of Sperlonga and Gaeta. To the southeast the Castelli Romani offer a fine combination of history and gastronomy, while to the northwest the tombs of the Etruscans are waiting to be discovered. Viterbo, to the north, offers medieval charm, hot springs and Renaissance architectural extravagances, while you can only marvel at the extensive ruins of Hadrian's villa to the northeast. Stopping for lunch at a local trattoria or selecting ingredients for a gourmet picnic is half the fun. But beware if you are driving, especially on Sundays. Romans are addicted to what they refer to as the *gita fuori porta* or day trip out of town and the traffic returning from these outings can be a nightmare.

> '...[the Campagne Romana] is the aptest and fittest burial ground for the Dead City. So sad, so quiet, so secret in its covering up of great masses of ruin.'

CHARLES DICKENS
Pictures from Italy (1846)

ARICCIA: PALAZZO CHIGI

Alessandro Chigi was the pope who gave Rome its baroque face. This was his summer retreat, the centre-piece of Bernini's exercise in town-planning that is Ariccia. Sold by the Chigi family in the 1980s and opened to the public since 1999, his *palazzo* (built in 1672) has been restored to its original pale-blue colour and is full of historical paintings and furniture. Worth noting are the pharmacy, with miniature portraits of the family from the 16th century onwards, and the *Salada Pranzo d'Estate*.

➕ Off map
✉ Piazza di Corte, 14
☎ 06 933 0053
🕐 Tours: Tue–Fri 11.30, 4.30, 5.30, Sat–Sun 10–7 on the hour
🚌 COTRAL bus from Anagnina to Ariccia or from terminal to Albano Laziale then bus

BOMARZO

The *Sacro Bosco* or *Parco dei Mostri* (Park of Monsters) at Bomarzo near Viterbo was created in the mid-1500s by Prince Vicino Orsini. While other nobles were building refined villas and laying out Renaissance gardens, the prince employed anonymous sculptors who crafted grotesque figures, including a life-size elephant crushing a Roman soldier with its trunk and a screaming face with a mouth big enough to hold several people. Inscriptions encourage today's visitors to 'eat, drink and be merry for after death there is no pleasure'. It was a favourite with the painter Salvador Dali.

➕ Off map
✉ Sacro Bosco, 01020 Bomarzo (VT)
☎ (0761) 924029
🕐 Apr–end Sep daily 8.30–6.30; Oct–end Mar 8.30–5
🍴 Restaurant, bar
🚌 COTRAL bus from Saxa Rubra to Viterbo, then to Bomarzo.
💰 Expensive
↔ Viterbo (➤ 90)

ROME EXCURSIONS

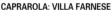

CAPRAROLA: VILLA FARNESE ✪

Off map

✉ Piazza Farnese

☎ (0761) 646052

🕐 Tue–Sun 9–6.30, (closes at 4 Oct–end Mar)

🚌 COTRAL bus from Saxa Rubra to Caprarola.
By car: 80km (50 miles) SS2 bis (Cassia bis) from Rome, then SS2 to Sutri, then follow signs to Caprarola

♿ None 💷 Inexpensive

Villa Farnese

One of the high points of Italian Mannerism, the imposing Villa Farnese, built by Antonio di Sangallo the Younger for Pierluigi Farnese, dwarfs the little town of Caprarola. Cardinal Alessandro Farnese took up residence in 1559, hiring one of the most competent architects of the late Renaissance, Vignola, to modify his home. Retaining the original and unusual pentagonal floor plan, Vignola turned the entire town of Caprarola into a setting for the palace, raising and extending the approach road and burying the lower storeys of the existing houses.

The *piano nobile* is the only floor open to the public. It is approached by Vignola's monumental spiral staircase of stone columns and frescoes up which Alessandro Farnese

used to ride on his horse. Frescoes recording significant moments in the Farnese family history decorate all the rooms, except for the *Sala del Mappamondo*, where there are instead huge paintings of maps of the world (as it was known in the 16th century) and wonderful frescoes of constellations on the ceiling. The gardens outside are also worth a close look.

CERVETERI ✪✪

🗺 81A2

Banditaccia Necropolis/ Museo Nazionale di Cerveteri

☎ 06 994 0001

🕐 Banditaccia Necropolis: Tue–Sun 8.30 to 1 hour before sunset. Museo Nazionale di Cerveteri: Tue–Sun 8.30–7.30

🚌 COTRAL bus from Lepanto

🚆 From Termini, Tiburtina, Ostiense or Trastevere to Cerveteri-Ladispoli station (6km/4 miles from centre)

🚌 Local bus runs from main piazza in Cerveteri to necropolis in summer only. **By car**: 44km (27 miles) by A12 or Via Aurelia (SS1)

💷 Necropolis and museum moderate

Founded by the Etruscans in the 8th century BC, ancient Caere was one of the great trading centres of the Mediterranean between the 7th and 5th centuries BC. In the **Banditaccia Necropolis**, a couple of kilometres from the main piazza of modern Cerveteri, the tombs of the inhabitants of the prosperous city are laid out in the form of a town, with streets and squares—a real city of the dead.

A map on sale at the entrance to the necropolis, which is set among Roman pines and cypress trees, is a useful guide to the tombs. Do not miss the 6th-century Tomba dei Capitelli carved from light volcanic rock to resemble Etruscan houses and the Tomba dei Rilievi decorated with painted reliefs of cooking utensils and other household objects. The Tomba degli Scudi e delle Sedie outside the main gate has chairs carved out of the tufo and unusual reliefs of shields decorating the walls.

The **Museo Nazionale di Cerveteri** in the town centre displays interesting pottery and sarcophagi from Cerveteri and the nearby port of Pyrgi, although most of the best discoveries are in the Vatican Museums (▶ 24) and Villa Giulia (▶ 78).

Etruria

Although little remains of Etruscan cities in the area of northern Lazio referred to as Etruria, many tombs, which contained reproductions of their occupants' luxuries and favourite things, have survived and give a fascinating insight into Etruscan civilisation. The Etruscans were clever, perhaps too clever for their own good. One historical account tells the story of an Etruscan man who set off for Gaul with his belongings and ample quantities of good wine. The precious nectar convinced the Gauls to come down to Italy, where they subsequently wiped out the Etruscan race.

Head out of Rome on the Via Aurelia (SS1), which joins the autostrada A12. After a visit to the necropolis of Cerveteri (▶ 82), continue north up the A12.

Civitavecchia, one of Rome's ports, is worth a detour. Established by Emperor Trajan in AD106, the town regained importance as a papal stronghold in the 16th century, when Michelangelo designed the fortress.

Continuing on the A12 up the coast you reach Tarquinia.

This is thought to have been founded in the 12th century BC, an important economic and political centre for the Etruscans. The painted tombs at the necropolis of Monterozzi are a must. The Museo Nazionale di Tarquinia has a collection of artefacts.

Turn right onto a minor road after Tarquinia and head inland for about 20km (12 miles) until you reach Tuscania.

This became a leading Etruscan city after the 4th century BC. Lovely sarcophagi are on display in the Museo Archeologico. However it is the post-Etruscan civilisation which makes an impression—especially the churches of San Pietro and Santa Maria Maggiore, built in the 8th century AD with 11th- and 12th-century additions.

Return to Rome by the same route or taking the Via Cassia (SS2) from Vetralla to Rome.

Distance
230km (143 miles)

Time
1 day

Start/end point
Rome
✚ 28C3

Lunch
Le Due Orfanelle (€€)
✉ Via di Porta Tarquinia 11a, Tarquinia
☎ (0766) 856307
🕐 Closed Tue

The Roman aqueduct at Tarquinia

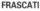
FRASCATI ⭐

Situated 25km (16 miles) from Rome, Frascati is the nearest of the Castelli Romani—the towns dotted along the volcanic Alban Hills. Frascati suffered severe damage during World War II, but many of the buildings have been restored, including the cathedral of San Pietro in Piazza San Pietro and the church of the Gesù designed by Pietro da Cortona, which is decorated with fresco perspectives.

Frascati is renowned for both its white wine (this can be sampled fresh from the barrel in the numerous cellars around the town) and its Renaissance villas. The magnificent **Villa Aldobrandini**, designed by Giacomo della Porta between 1598 and 1603 for Cardinal Pietro Aldobrandini, a nephew of Pope Clement VIII, dominates the town. On a clear day the views of Rome from the terrace can be breathtaking.

Frascati, with other Castelli towns, was once part of the ancient city of Tusculum, which dates back as far as the 9th century BC. It was a favourite spot for Roman dignitaries, many of whom had villas there. The archaeological remains of Tusculum are scant: there is a Roman road leading up to the former city, the ruins of the villa of Emperor Tiberius and—best-preserved of all—a small amphitheatre now somewhat notorious after reports of black masses being held there. For directions refer to Castelli Romani drive (▶ 85).

➕ 81C2

ℹ️ Frascati tourist office (✉️ Piazza Marconi 1, Frascati ☎️ 06 942 0331)

Villa Aldobrandini

✉️ Piazza G. Marconi, Frascati

☎️ 06 942 0331

🕐 Mon–Fri 9–1, 3–6 (closes at 5 Oct–end Mar)

🚉 Train from Termini station, 30 min. **By car:** Via Tuscolana from Rome for about 25km (16 miles)

👜 Free (the tourist office in Piazza G. Marconi issues passes to the garden of Villa Aldobrandini)

Renaissance villas of Frascati

Castelli Romani

The Castelli Romani are small towns which grew up in ancient times and developed during the Middle Ages along the slopes of the Alban Hills. The name probably comes from the palaces built there by popes and noble Roman families. Each has its own history and attractions.

From Frascati's Piazza G. Marconi, follow the signs to Tusculum (➤ 84).

Grottaferrata is 3km (2 miles) south of Frascati and is famous for its 11th-century abbey. Castelli wines are high on the list of popular Italian table wines. Even in Roman times they were regarded as 'unstable'. Today locals insist that the wine is better drunk on the spot. Test the theory by quaffing from the barrel in the wine shops in the towns.

Following route 215, you reach Marino, whose white wine is regarded as the region's best after Frascati. From Marino the scenic Via dei Laghi runs along the eastern rim of Lago Albano. Just after the lake, turn left on SS218 to Monte Cavo (the second highest of the Alban Hills) and Rocca di Papa, at 680m (2,230ft).

This is the highest of the Castelli towns and one of the most picturesque with its medieval quarter.

Return to Via dei Laghi until the turnoff on the right to Nemi. Nemi, positioned above the volcanic lake of the same name, is famous for its wild strawberries. It is an attractive place that gets busy at weekends. On the other side of Lake Nemi the panoramic SS7 continues to Genzano di Roma, Ariccia and Albano Laziale.

Ariccia is renowned for its main square ornamented by Bernini and for its *porchetta*, or stuffed roast pork. Albano Laziale has majestic Etruscan and Roman ruins.

From Albano Laziale take the picturesque Galleria di Sopra to Castel Gandolfo.

This is the summer residence of the Pope. He gives a blessing every Sunday, June to September.

Return to Rome on the Via Appia Antica.

Distance
90km (59 miles)

Time
Half a day

Start/end point
Rome
✚ 81C2

Lunch
Zarazá (€–€€) (➤ 99)
✉ Viale Regina Margherita
   45, Frascati
☎ 06 942 2053
🕐 Closed Mon and Sun eve

85

81A1
☎ 06 5635 8099
🕐 Apr–end Sep Tue–Sun
9–6; Oct–end Mar
Tue–Sun 9–4
🍴 Il Monumento (€€)
(➤ 99)
✉ Piazza Umberto I 18
☎ 06 565 0021
🕐 Closed Mon
🚇 Metro B to Piramide, thn
trains from adjoining
railway station every
10–30 minutes to Ostia
Antica. **By car**: 25km (16
miles). Via del Mare (SS8
bis) from Rome
✋ Moderate

*Visit Ostia Antica's
famously well-preserved
Roman town for a good
idea of what life was like
in Italy BC*

OSTIA ANTICA ✪✪✪

Founded at the mouth of the river Tiber by the Romans in the 4th century BC, Ostia Antica was the port of ancient Rome. Populated by merchants and sailors, the city was a strategically important centre of defence and trade until its decline in the 4th century AD.

After Pompeii and Herculaneum, Ostia Antica is the best-preserved Roman town in Italy. Its park-like setting is a refreshing change from the chaos of Rome, and should be enjoyed at a leisurely pace. Allow a good few hours to explore the **excavations** which are as fascinating (if not quite so grand) as those at the Roman Forum and give a good impression of what day-to-day life in a working Roman town was like.

The ruins span both sides of the kilometre-long main street, the Decumanus Maximus, from the Porta Romana to the Porta Marina at the other end (which once opened on to the seafront). On the right just after the Porta Romana are the Terme di Nettuno (baths of Neptune), best viewed by climbing the stone stairs at the front. Further on is the impressive amphitheatre which could hold 2,700 people. It was restored in 1927 and is used as a theatre in summer (➤ 113). Behind the theatre is the town's commercial centre, Piazzale delle Corporazioni, surrounded by offices and shops with decorative mosaics announcing the trades practised by each business.

Returning to the Decumanus Maximus, the ruins of the forum are to the left. Off to the right are the remains of some *horrea* (warehouses) that once stood all over the city. Also on the right is the well-preserved Casa di Diana and the *Thermopilium*, a Roman bar complete with a marble counter and frescoes of the available fare. Just beyond, to the northeast, is the museum which houses statues, mosaics and other artefacts found at the site.

Before you leave, look at the medieval *borgo* (village) of Ostia, a stone's throw from the archaeological site, where there are some characteristic cottages which once housed workers from the nearby salt plains and a fortified castle built for future Pope Julius II in 1483–6.

SPERLONGA ✪

With its whitewashed houses and narrow streets, the popular resort town of Sperlonga, built on a high, rocky promontory on the coast south of Terracina, is possibly more Greek than Italian in feel. Cars are banned from the old centre, which is made up of winding alleys and stone stairways. In the summer the spectacular beach is filled with wealthy Romans vying for a place in the front row of the beach-umbrella/sunbed operations (there is a small stretch of non-paying public beach but this seems to get smaller every year). Food and drink can be bought from the many beachside bars.

The archaeological museum located 2km (1mile) from the town displays artefacts found among the ruins of the nearby villa of Emperor Tiberius, including reconstructions of larger-than-life-size sculpture groups illustrating the adventures of Ulysses, erected between AD4 and 26 for Tiberius in his nearby cliff-face grotto.

Picturesque Sperlonga has a harbour as well as a very popular beach

➕ Off map
🍴 Lido da Rocco (€–€€)
  ✉ Via Spiaggia Angelo 22 ☎ (0771) 548493
🚉 Naples train from Termini station to Fondi
🚌 Local bus to Sperlonga from Fondi should coincide with the train. Taxis also available. The return bus leaves from the central piazza at the top of the hill. **By car**: 120km (74 miles). Take the SS148 south out of Rome (follow signs to Latina and Terracina). From Terracina take the SS213 to Sperlonga

The delightful grounds of Tivoli's Villa d'Este offer respite from the summer heat

TIVOLI ⭐⭐

Tivoli was a country retreat for Roman patricians and a summer playground for the monied classes during the Renaissance. The town has long been famous for its Travertine marble and the quarries that line the road from Rome testify to this continuing flourishing trade. Easily reached by car or public transportation, Tivoli is one of the most popular day trips from Rome. The Villa d'Este and Villa Adriana are the best-known sights, but it is worth having a look at the Rocca Pia, a 15th-century castle built by Pope Pius II at the top of the town, and wandering around the labyrinthine streets of the historical centre, stopping at the Romanesque church of San Silvestro (where there are some interesting early medieval frescoes) and the 17th-century cathedral of San Lorenzo.

There is a sense of faded splendour about the Renaissance pleasure palace **Villa d'Este** created in 1550 by Cardinal Ippolito d'Este, grandson of Borgia Pope Alexander VI. Some of the remaining Mannerist frescoes in the villa have been restored and deserve a look, but the residence is totally upstaged by the gardens—an almost entirely symmetrical series of terraces, shady pathways and spectacular fountains, powered solely by gravitational force and including one that once played the organ and another that imitated the call of birds. Sadly neither of these are functional today, but you can still get a sense of the fantastic creation that the garden once was, and there are delightful features such as the long terrace of grotesque heads, all spouting water, and the Rometta fountain (on the far left going down the terraces) which has reproductions of Rome's major buildings. From 1865 to 1886 the villa was home to Franz Liszt and inspired his *Fountains of the Villa d'Este*.

The waterfalls and gardens of Tivoli's **Villa Gregoriana** were created when Pope Gregory XVI diverted the flow of the Aniene river to put an end to the periodic flooding in the area. There are two main waterfalls: the large Grande Cascata on the far side and a smaller one at the neck of the gorge, designed by Bernini. Shady paths surrounded by lush vegetation wind down to various viewpoints over the waterfalls and across to two exceptionally well-preserved Roman temples, the circular Temple of Vesta and the rectangular Temple of the Sibyl, which date from the Republican era.

✚ 81C2

🍴 Ristorante Antiche Terme di Diana (€€)
  ✉ Via dei Sosii 6, Tivoli
  ☎ (0774) 335239
  🕐 Closed Mon

🚍 Metro to Rebibbia, then COTRAL bus to Tivoli. Buses leave every 10 minutes (Mon–Sat), 15–20 minutes (Sun).
  By car: 40km (25 miles) east of Rome on Via Tiburtina SS5 or Rome-L'Aquila autostrada A24

Villa d'Este
✉ Piazza Trento
☎ (0774) 312070
🕐 Apr–end Sep Tue–Sun 9–7.30; Oct–end Mar Tue–Sun 9 to 1 hour before dusk
💰 Expensive

Villa Gregoriana
✉ Largo S. Angelo
☎ (0774) 311249 (tourist office)
🕐 Due to open 2005; check with tourist office for opening details.

VILLA ADRIANA ✪✪✪

Constructed between AD118 and 134, Villa Adriana was the largest and most sumptuous villa ever built in the Roman Empire. It was the country palace of Emperor Hadrian and later used by other emperors. After the fall of the empire it was plundered for building materials. Many of its decorations were used to embellish the Villa d'Este.

A model near the entrance gives you some idea of the scale of the complex. The site is enormous and you will need several hours to see it properly. Hadrian travelled widely and was a keen architect, and parts of the villa were inspired by buildings he had seen around the world. The massive *Pecile*, through which you enter, was a reproduction of a building in Athens and the Canopus, on the far side of the site, is a copy of the sanctuary of Serapis near Alexandria, and the long canal of water, originally surrounded by Egyptian statues, reproducing the Nile.

Highlights include the fishpond (probably used less for keeping fish than for creating reflections and plays of light) encircled by an underground gallery where the emperor took his walks, the baths, and Hadrian's private retreat, the Teatro Marittimo, a small circular palace on an island in a pool, which could be reached only by a retractable bridge. There are *nymphaeums*, temples, barracks and a museum. Archaeologists have found features such as a heated bench with steam pipes under the sand, and a network of subterranean service passages for horses and carts.

🟥 81C2
✉ Via di Villa Adriana, Tivoli
☎ (0774) 530203
🕐 Daily 9 to 1 hour before dusk. Tickets sold until one hour before closing
🍴 Adriano (€€–€€€)
　✉ Via di Villa Adriana 194 ☎ (0774) 382235
　🕐 Closed Sun dinner
🚌 32km (20 miles). Local bus from Tivoli's Piazza Garibaldi to Villa Adriana. COTRAL bus can drop you on main road to Rome (1km/half a mile) to villa).
♿ Expensive

In its day, the Villa Adriana, built by Emperor Hadrian, was the most lavish of its kind

🔲 Off map
ℹ️ Viterbo tourist office
(✉ Piazza San Carluccio,
Viterbo ☎ (0761)
304795)
🍽 Richiastro (€) ✉ Via
Della Marrocca 16–18
☎ (0761) 228009
🕐 Closed Mon–Wed,
Sun eve
🚌 COTRAL bus from Saxa
Rubra station to Viterbo.
🚆 From Termini station
(also Tiburtina, Ostiense,
Trastevere stations) to
Viterbo (2 hours). **By car:**
Cassia bis (SS2 bis) from
Rome 110km/68 miles
(1½ hours). Pay parking.

*San Pellegrino, the oldest
quarter of medieval
Viterbo, is often used for
film locations*

VITERBO ✪✪✪

Founded by the Etruscans and later taken over by Rome, Viterbo developed into an important medieval centre and in the 13th century became the residence of the popes. Although badly bombed during World War II, it remains Lazio's best preserved medieval town and its historical quarter, San Pellegrino, is such a perfect architectural ensemble that it is often used as a movie set. The natural hot springs close by are an additional attraction.

From the rather oddly named but lovely Piazza della Morte (Death Square) a bridge leads over to Piazza San Lorenzo and the black-and-white striped cathedral of the same name which dates from the 12th century. Inside are magnificent cosmati tiled floors and the tomb of Pope John XXI, who died in 1277 when the floor of his room collapsed. Next door is the 13th-century Palazzo Papale. Have a peek at the 'new' roof. The original one was removed in 1271, during the first conclave in Viterbo, to speed up the election of the pope. The cardinals, slow to elect the new pontiff, were locked inside the palace, next the roof was removed and finally, in desperation, the cardinals were put on a starvation diet. It was 33 months before Gregory X was finally elected.

The pretty Romanesque church of Santa Maria Nuova, with its outdoor pulpit from which St. Thomas Aquinas preached and its cloister at the back, is also worth a look, before you head up towards Piazza del Plebiscito, which is dominated by the 16th-century Palazzo Comunale. Stop for a rest in Piazza delle Erbe by the fountain or for refreshments at the 15th-century Caffe Schenardi.

Where To...

Eat and Drink	92–99
Stay	100–103
Shop	104–109
Take the Children	110–111
Be Entertained	112–116

Above: *Nightlife Roman style*
Right: *Documents inside the Keats-Shelley Memorial House*

Rome

How Much will it Cost?

The price brackets used here are for a three-course meal for one without drinks or service—a half litre of house wine will often not make that much difference to the bill especially in cheaper places:

€ = up to €20
€€ = €20–€40
€€€ = more than €40

The bill will usually include a small cover charge (about €1–2 per person) and some restaurants add service (10–15 per cent); otherwise tipping is usually about 10 per cent.

Agata e Romeo (€€€)

Near the Basilica of Santa Maria Maggiore, this intimate, elegant restaurant is renowned for its cozy and convivial atmosphere, its excellent Roman and southern Italian dishes, and equally a wine list that pays tribute to the quality of the food.

✉ Via Carlo Alberto 45
☎ 06 446 6115 🕐 Closed Sat, Sun 🚇 Vittorio Emanuele
🚌 70, 71, 360 to Via Carlo Alberto

Alberto Ciarla (€€€)

The classic Rome restaurant for serious fish lovers—fresh fish in its stark simplicity or as a sublimely creative dish, accompanied by a perfect match from the extensive wine list. There are intimate candlelit tables, a dramatic red-and-black decor, and refined and impeccable service.

✉ Piazza San Cosimato 40
☎ 06 581 8668 🕐 Closed Sun, lunch 🚌 8, 630, 780 to Viale di Trastevere

Alfredo a Via Gabi (€€)

Comfortable local trattoria with pavement tables for outside eating in summer. Traditional and innovative specialties from Rome and the Marches, Roman dishes, especially on Saturday. A family atmosphere and cordial, attentive service. Remember to reserve on weekends.

✉ Via Gabi 36/8 ☎ 06 7720 6792 🕐 Closed Tue 🚇 Re di Roma 🚌 87, 360

Augusto (€)

This historic Roman trattoria has characteristic paper-covered tables (outside in summer). Happy confusion reigns here and service may be slapdash but the Roman cooking is genuine. Go early to enjoy the best dishes.

✉ Piazza de' Renzi 15
☎ 06 580 3798 🕐 Closed Sun
🚌 To Piazza Sonnino

Il Bacaro (€€)

A candle-lit romantic little restaurant especially popular with young people both for its atmosphere and its location (near the Pantheon). It is particularly appealing in summer with outside tables. Innovative Italian dishes and affable service. Extensive wine list.

✉ Via degli Spagnoli 27
☎ 06 686 4110 🕐 Closed Sun
🚌 To Largo di Torre Argentina

Da Baffetto (€)

Immensely popular central pizzeria, recognizable from afar due to the crowd jostling to get past the door. Service however is swift and efficient, the pizzas are well worth the wait. Not a place for lingering. Open late.

✉ Via del Governo Vecchio 114 ☎ 06 686 1617 🕐 Closed lunch 🚌 To Corso Vittorio Emanuele

Binario 4 (€)

A welcome arrival near the Colosseum: an updated version of the genuine local 'osteria'. There are carefully executed traditional dishes itemized daily on a strategically placed blackboard. Informal bonhomie. No rules for eating—have as little or as much as you like. Open late.

✉ Via San Giovanni in Laterano 32 ☎ 06 700 5561
🕐 Always open 🚇 Colosseo
🚌 To Piazza del Colosseo

La Bottecilla (€€)
Cheerful home-from-home tiny welcoming trattoria with good plain regional Italian cooking with unexpected individual touches. Delicious homemade desserts. Some tables outside in summer. Excellent wine list.

✉ Vicolo del Leopardo 39a ☎ 06 581 4738 🕔 Closed Wed, Mon–Sat lunch 🚌 To Piazza Sonnino

Cecilia Metella (€€)
At the top of a winding drive, a shower of tables in a delightful garden setting, complete with fountain. Large, open-fire interior for winter. Cheerful, bustling waiters. Stress-free parking.

✉ Via Appia Antica 125–129 ☎ 06 513 6743 🕔 Closed Mon 🚌 118

Al Ceppo (€€)
Skilfully recreated regional dishes from the Marches alongside creative variations on more local dishes are to be savoured in this elegant salon that has long enjoyed the exacting patronage of its local Parioli regulars. There is also a discerning wine list.

✉ Via Panama 2/4 ☎ 06 841 9696 🕔 Closed Mon and 2 weeks Aug 🚌 To Piazza Ungheria

Checchino dal 1887 (€€€)
In the heart of Testaccio, this cool vaulted restaurant vaunts the experience of over 100 years. Quintessential Roman cuisine based on the once lowly offerings from the old slaughterhouse opposite. A superb natural wine cellar complements the meal.

✉ Via di Monte Testaccio 30 ☎ 06 574 6318 🕔 Closed Sun, Mon 🚇 Piramide 🚌 3, 60, 75, 118

Ciak (€€)
A rustic Tuscan bistro for lovers of game, roast meats and inimitable local specialties: checked tablecloths, engaging informal service, enthusiastic diners, friendly seating arrangements and an open grill all add to the enjoyment.

✉ Vicolo del Cinque 21 ☎ 06 589 4774 🕔 Closed Mon, lunch 🚌 To Piazza Sonnino

Colline Emiliane (€€)
An old-fashioned family trattoria just off Piazza Barberini, which adheres strictly to the well-established genuine traditions of the rich cuisine of the northern region of Emilia Romagna. Excellent homemade pasta, particularly *tortellini*, boiled meats and no frills.

✉ Via degli Avignonesi 22 ☎ 06 481 7538 🕔 Closed Fri and Aug 🚇 Barberini 🚌 To Piazza Barberini

Il Convivio (€€€)
A prime choice for a special occasion: creative cuisine spiced with a touch of genius and true professionalism. Both the well-balanced set menus and the *à la carte* dishes are tantalizing in their range and variety; a comparable wine list.

✉ Vicolo dei Soldati 31 ☎ 06 686 9432 🕔 Closed Sun dinner 🚌 To Corso del Rinascimento

Ditirambo (€€)
The two beamed rooms with tiled floors have the tranquillity of an old country inn; innovative Italian dishes are based on genuine ingredients and subtle combinations. Homemade bread, pasta and desserts; excellent (house) wine. Informative staff.

✉ Piazza della Cancelleria 74 ☎ 06 687 1626 🕔 Closed Mon 🚌 To Corso Vittorio Emanuele

Opening and Closing
In general, restaurants are open for lunch from about 12 until 3 and from about 8 until 11 for dinner. Most remain closed one day a week and many are closed two or more weeks in August and/or for up to a month in November or January, on Christmas day, Labour Day (1 May) and other public holidays.

What to Eat

A full Italian lunch or dinner starts with *antipasti* (raw and cooked vegetables, cold meats, sea-food) followed by the *primo* (first) course of pasta, rice or soup. *Secondi* are the main courses of meat or fish accompanied, or followed, by *contorni* (vegetables and salad). The meal finishes with *dolce* and coffee with digestive liqueurs. Although you do not have to eat your way through all of these, most restaurants expect you to have at least a couple of courses.

Ecce Bombo (€)

Gingham tablecoths and dark wood panelling give a rustic feel to this relaxed restaurant. Innovative modern Italian dishes include tasty combinations such as kiwi chicken. Tables outside on busy street provide good people watching.

✉ Via Tor Millina ☎ 06 6680 3469 🕐 Always open 🚍 To Corso Vittorio Emanuele

Enoteca Corsi (€)

An old-fashioned and comfortable central spot for a plain and simple lunch. No pretensions here—genuine Roman food, informal service and friendly diners eager to share their table space. Informal service. Adjoining wine shop also recommended.

✉ Via del Gesù 87/8 ☎ 06 679 0821 🕐 Closed Sun, eves 🚍 To Largo di Torre Argentina

Est! Est! Est! dei Fratelli Ricci (€)

Subdued but much loved central pizzeria with neither brashness nor pretensions. Diners will find simple wooden tables, minimal decor, excellent flat and crispy Roman pizzas, tap beer and regional Italian wines. An experience.

✉ Via Genova 32 ☎ 06 488 1107 🕐 Closed Mon, lunch 🚇 Repubblica 🚍 To Piazza della Repubblica

Fiaschetteria Beltramme (€€)

Try to get here early after a shopping trip. A nostalgic survivor of past glories, this tiny trattoria is beginning to suffer from too much superstar visibility, so catch the lingering atmosphere. Share your table, jostle with the famous and enjoy genuine Roman cooking in suitably uninhibited cramped conditions.

✉ Via della Croce 39

None 🕐 Closed Sun 🚇 Spagna 🚍 To Via del Corso

Gioia mia (Pisciapiano) (€)

A useful spot after a hard day's shopping, offering menus for all palates and purses: from pizzas to full-blown meals. Noisy and chaotic but enjoyable nonetheless. (*Pisciapiano*, for those with linguistic curiosity, actually refers to a Tuscan wine with diuretic qualities, hence the emblematic cherub relieving himself.)

✉ Via degli Avignonesi 34 ☎ 06 488 2784 🕐 Closed Sun 🚇 Barberini 🚍 To Piazza Barberini

Grappolo d'Oro (€)

A stone's throw from Campo de' Fiori, this pleasant trattoria continues to offer typical basic Roman fare at prices that are more than reasonable for such a location. Discreet, cordial service and guaranteed satisfaction.

✉ Piazza della Cancelleria 80 ☎ 06 689 7080 🕐 Always open 🚍 To Corso Vittorio Emanuele

'Gusto (€–€€)

A chic, minimalist ambience opened in the 1990s and so loved by the Romans. Downstairs its piazzas and salads, upstairs the restaurant combines Italian traditions with sitr-fry Eastern cooking. Saturday and Sunday brunch served 11.30–3.30. Be prepared for lunch-time office crowds.

✉ Piazza Augusto Imperatore 9 ☎ 06 322 6273 🕐 Closed Mon 🚍 To Piazza Augusto Impratore

Hostaria Antica Roma (€€€€)

A pleasant stop on the Appian Way and attractively illuminated by candlelight for dinner. Specialties include gnocchi with clams, fillet of bass with herbs and beef fillet with truffles. A 2,000-year old recipe is used for the flan dish. Other ancient Roman dishes are a feature on Tuesdays and Thursdays.

📩 **Via Appia Antica 87** ☎ **06 513 2888** 🕔 **Closed Mon** 🚌 **118**

Ivo a Trastevere (€)
Go early to avoid the evening queue, as this is the best known of Trastevere's pizzerias. Enjoy a classic Roman pizza and join the scores of contented customers who can say that they have eaten at this institution. Polluted tables outside for those who are non-environmentalists. Open late.

📩 **Via San Francesco a Ripa 158** ☎ **06 581 7082** 🕔 **Closed Tue, lunch** 🚌 **To Piazza Sonnino, Viale Trastevere**

Lorodinapoli (€€)
This popular Neapolitan restaurant is based on an astute winning formula: a concise lunch menu and an inspirational evening one, which changes every day according to available ingredients and the creativity of the chef. It's essential to reserve ahead to ensure a table. Open late.

📩 **Via Fabio Massimo 101** ☎ **06 323 5790** 🕔 **Closed Sun** Ⓜ **Ottaviano** 🚌 **To Piazza del Risorgimento**

Da Lucia (€)
Catch the last glimpses of the fading splendours of one of old Trastevere's culinary historic spots. Genuine Roman dishes are traditionally and carefully prepared and served without undue ceremony, as is the wine. Sit outside in summer and take in the local atmosphere.

📩 **Vicolo del Mattonato 2b**

131c2

☎ **06 580 3601** 🕔 **Closed Mon** 🚌 **To Piazza Sonnino**

Il Margutta (€–€€)
A good vegetarian restaurant and a place to drop in, at any time of day, for a drink, a snack or a complete meal. Good selection of Mediterranean vegetable dishes and a recommended delicate *fritto misto*. You can dine outside in fine weather.

📩 **Via Margutta 118** ☎ **06 3265 0577** 🕔 **Always open** Ⓜ **Flaminio** 🚌 **To Piazzale Flaminio**

Navona Notte (€)
Popular with locals for many years and known for its excellent pasta and some of the largest and tastiest pizza in Rome. Excellent value for money and in a good position near Piazza Navona. Check out the Tempieto della Pace church around the corner, superbly lit at night.

📩 **Via del Teatro Pace 44** ☎ **06 686 9278** 🚌 **To Corso Vittorio Emanuele** 130/c3-c4

Nerone (€–€€)
Close to the Colosseum, this small, friendly trattoria is a pleasant spot for an inexpensive and relaxed meal. The *antipasti* is especially good, to be followed by Roman and Abruzzese specialties. A few tables for outside dining.

📩 **Via delle Terme di Tito 96** ☎ **06 481 7952** 🕔 **Closed Sun** 🚌 **To Piazza del Colosseo**

News Cafe (€)
More than just an internet café, the News Cafe provides newspapers in ten different languages and helps you keep abreast with world affairs via 24-hour TV. Sit outside and you get a good salad or pasta dish too. Close to Trevi fountain

📩 **Via della Stamperia 72** ☎ **06 6992 3473** 🚌 **To Via del Tritone** 131/Ex 134/A5

Piatti di Buon Ricordo
Some restaurants take part in the *piatto del buon ricordo* (literally, 'plate of good memory') scheme, in which anybody ordering the special dish of the house will be presented with a plate to take home with them. At Agata e Romeo, for example, the *piatto del buon ricordo* is *pasta e broccoli in brodo di arzilla* (pasta and broccoli).

Snacking

Rome has several eating alternatives if you are in a hurry or only want a snack. *Enoteche* (wine bars) often have cheeses, cold meats and sometimes pasta dishes to accompany their wine lists. *Birrerie* sell beer and basic dishes such as hamburgers. *Pizza al taglio* sell slices of freshly made pizza to take away. Bars have sandwiches and sometimes a *tavola calda*, with one or two hot *primi* and *secondi*. Finally, *alimentari* (grocers) fill rolls with whatever is in stock.

Otello alla Concordia (€€)

After some serious shopping in the busy Via del Corso relax in the attractive 18th-century courtyard of this family-run restaurant. Typical Roman fare accompanied by some local wine. Book for outside tables.

✉ **Via della Croce 81** ☎ **06 679 1178** Ⓒ **Closed Sun** Ⓜ **Spagna** 🚌 **To Via del Corso**

Panattoni (€)

A hugely popular Trastevere pizzeria nicknamed 'the coffin-maker' (*cassamortaro*) for its characteristic marble-topped tables. Watch the chef's flamboyant flipping of pizzas at the large oven inside, scramble for an outside table in summer.

✉ **Viale Trastevere 53** ☎ **06 580 0919** Ⓒ **Closed Wed, lunch** 🚌 **To Viale Trastevere**

Papà Baccus (€€)

An eminently reliable welcoming restaurant in the often daunting Via Veneto area. From his native mountainous Tuscany, the owner offers traditional country soups, ham, salami, grilled meats and fish, and delicious homemade desserts. Informal service, seats outside in summer.

✉ **Via Toscana 36** ☎ **06 4274 2808** Ⓒ **Closed Sat lunch, Sun** Ⓜ **Barberini** 🚌 **To Via Vittorio Veneto**

Da Paris (€€)

Satisfied customers who return again and again to this elegant restaurant attest to the winning formula of Trastevere's prime Roman-Jewish restaurant: unchanging traditional dishes and a sapient use of fresh ingredients. Delicate *vegetable fritto misto*, fresh fish. Small terrace in front, lofty rooms within. Well-selected wine list.

✉ **Piazza San Calisto 7a**

☎ **06 581 5378** Ⓒ **Closed Sun eve, Mon** 🚌 **To Viale Trastevere**

Pasquilino (€€)

This long-established trattoria is only a few minutes' walk east of the Colosseum, and serves large portions of good simple food.

✉ **Via dei Santi Quattro 66** ☎ **06 700 0576** Ⓒ **Closed Mon and 2 weeks Aug** Ⓜ **Colosseo** 🚌 **To Piazza del Colosseo**

Peccati di Gola (€€)

Set in a scenic quiet piazza of Trastevere, and particularly atmospheric in summer, this elegant little restaurant (aptly named after culinary over-indulgence) specializes in Mediterranean and Calabrian fish dishes. Various reasonable set menus. Friendly, attentive service.

✉ **Piazza de' Ponziani 7a** ☎ **06 581 4529** Ⓒ **Closed Mon** 🚌 **To Viale Trastevere**

Perilli a Testaccio (€€)

A popular, noisy and crowded trattoria making no concessions to fashionable décor, thriving on its reputation for gargantuan portions of honest Roman specialties. Locals rub shoulders with the famous and everybody really enjoys themselves. Reservations essential.

✉ **Via Marmorata 39** ☎ **06 574 2415** Ⓒ **Closed Wed** Ⓜ **Piramide** 🚌 **To Via Marmorata**

Piperno (€€€)

At the heart of the Jewish Ghetto, the name Piperno has been synonymous with the best (and not cheap) Roman-Jewish cuisine for over 100 years. Time really does seem to stand still in this restaurant: the old-fashioned interior is a sombre backdrop, the waiters exude an olde-worlde chivalry and the classic food is consistently genuine. Reserve ahead.

✉ **Via Monte de' Cenci 9**
☎ **06 6880 2772** 🕐 **Closed Sun eve, Mon** 🚌 **To Via Arenula**

Pizzaré (€)

Worth a stop, especially at lunchtime, for true large-format Neapolitan pizzas in nearly 40 different combinations. Set menus at ludicrously low prices; also pasta, meat, salads and desserts.

✉ **Via di Ripetta 14**
☎ **06 321 1468** 🚌 **To Lungotevere in Augusta**

Trattoria Priscilla (€)

A useful place after trekking around the catacombs and one that is not hard on the pocket. Simple family-run trattoria offering classic Roman fare with no concessions to *haute cuisine* but happy to serve a good plate of pasta and a glass of wine.

✉ **Via Appia Antica 68**
☎ **06 513 6379** 🕐 **Closed Sun** 🚌 **118**

Nel Regno di Re Ferdinando II (€€€)

Located in Testaccio, this highly acclaimed Neapolitan restaurant serves all kinds of regional fish, meat and vegetable dishes and superb pizzas from the wood oven.

✉ **Via di Monte Testaccio 39**
☎ **06 578 3725** 🕐 **Always open** 🚇 **Piramide** 🚌 **To Via Marmorata**

Li Rioni (€)

An original street-like pizzeria, complete with tiled courtyard, streetlights and balconies. The atmosphere plus the excellent choice of pizzas have made it a local hot spot. It's very popular so you will have to be prepared to stand in line.

✉ **Via dei Santi Quattro 24**
☎ **06 7045 0605** 🕐 **Closed Tue** 🚌 **To Piazza del Colosseo**

Roma Sparita (€)

Located in a medieval square in Trastevere and dominated by the church of St. Cecilia, this restaurant serves genuine Roman cuisine with dishes such as beef strips with porcini mushrooms. Try the risotto with radicchio and walnuts. Pizzas are baked traditionally in a wood-burning oven. Excellent homemade desserts. Wash it down with wine from the Castelli Romana. Outside dining in summer.

✉ **Piazza S Cecilia 24** ☎ **06 580 0757** 🕐 **Closed Mon** 🚌 **To Viale di Trastevere**

Romolo nel Giardino della San Teodoro (€€€)

Stumble across this enticing and elegant little trattoria in its romantic setting and you will be treated to a memorable experience, especially in summer. Grilled meats, fresh fish and Roman specialties. Informal, welcoming. Good wines.

✉ **Via dei Fienili 49** ☎ **06 678 0933** 🕐 **Always open** 🚌 **To Piazza Bocca della Verità**

La Rosetta (€€€)

One of Rome's most famous fish restaurants located near the Pantheon. Dishes are simply prepared— but with flair and creativity—to retain the best of taste using only the freshest of ingredients. Try the lobster with herbs and cheese and red prawns with Sauterne and sage. Excellent wine list. The place to dress up and experience elegant dining. Reserve ahead.

✉ **Via della Rosetta 3–9**
☎ **06 686 1002** 🕐 **Closed Sun, Sat lunch** 🚌 **Piazza della Rotunda or Corso del Rinascimento**

Pizzas

The best pizzas have a hint of charcoal around the edges. This is caused by being cooked in wood ovens (*forno a legna*), which create temperatures that seem unbearable in summer. Not all pizzas are the same; Roman ones have a thin, crisp base while, in Naples, pizzas come on a thick, bready base, which is more filling; *calzone*, a particularly appetite-satisfying option, are made from folded over pizza dough stuffed with the filling you choose.

Rome & Excursions from the City

Vegetarians

In Rome there is a dearth of restaurants catering exclusively to vegetarians but that should not stop you from eating well. Even if you do not eat any animal products at all, wherever you go you are likely to find a good selection of delicious meat-, fish- and egg-free pasta dishes, which you can follow with a selection of vegetables (contorni) or cheese.

Sabatini (€€€)

Although no longer Rome's most famous restaurant, Sabatini, located in the lovely Piazza S. Maria in Trastevere, is still popular for its reliable food and lovely setting. The emphasis is on seafood; try the spaghetti with clams and the grilled fish in citronette. Outdoor patio. Reserving is essential.

✉ Piazza S Maria in Trastevere 13 ☎ 06 581 2026 🕐 Closed Wed, Aug 🚌 Piazza Sidney Sonnino, Lungotevere Sanzio

Risorante S Anna (€€)

Not far from the Campo de'Fiori, this is a lovely place to sample some excellent fresh fish and seafood. The appetizer buffet is a great way to start your meal to be followed by specialties that include the house pasta with mussels, clams, scampi and calamari all cooked in a spicy tomato sauce. In summer nothing can beat the strawberry tiramisú.

✉ Via di S Anna 8/9 ☎ 06 6830 7190 🕐 Closed Sun 🚌 To Corso Vittorio Emanuele II, Largo di Torre Argentina

Sitar (€–€€)

A quiet spot on the busy Via Cavour, this Indian restaurant features authentic fare from the Mughlai and Northern Indian regions. Among the most popular dishes are chicken tikka and butter or chilli chicken but also the 'tawa prantha' cuisine, usually reserved for family meals in India. It consists of naan bread baked on a griddle and stuffed with vegetables or meat. Good value set meals and options for vegetarians.

✉ Via Cavour 256a ☎ 06 488 4004 🚇 Cavour 🚌 To Via Cavour

Sora Lella (€€)

A legendary Roman institution on the enchanting Tiber Island, embued with the shades of Sora Lella, a charismatic Roman personality. The food is, naturally, Roman; the diners may be illustrious. Charming, informative service.

✉ Via del Ponte Quattro Capi 16 ☎ 06 686 1601 🕐 Closed Sun, Aug 🚌 To Lungotevere de'Cenci, Lungotevere Anguillare

Taverna Angelica (€€)

A restaurant near St. Peter's for romantic, intimate candle-lit dining until the small hours. Creative regional cuisine, both fish and meat, excellent cheeses and imaginative desserts (with well-matched dessert wines by the glass). Courteous and efficient service.

✉ Piazza delle Vaschette 14a ☎ 06 687 4514 🕐 Closed lunch 🚇 Ottaviano 🚌 To Piazza del Risorgimento

Taverna Cestia (€€)

A quality-for-money restaurant is popular with many of the foreign residents working for the nearby UN agency. An extensive menu of Italian dishes, competently executed, together with crisp Roman pizzas. Terrace outside.

✉ Viale Piramide Cestia 67 ☎ 06 574 3754 🕐 Closed Mon 🚇 Piramide 🚌 11, 13, 27, 30

La Taverna del Ghetto (€€)

A kosher restaurant located in the heart of Rome's

Jewish Ghetto in a 14th-century building. With a menu that changes every two weeks genuine Jewish Roman dishes are served here. Top of the menu are Jewish-style artichokes, homemade pasta, fresh fish, lamb and homemade cake.

✉ Via Portico d'Ottavia 8 ☎ 06 6880 9771 🕐 Closed Sat lunch, Fri dinner 🚌 To Largo di Torre Argentina

Vecchia Roma (€€€)
Unfussy but reliable cooking in a captivating 18th-century setting. The pretty piazza provides an ideal spot for alfresco dining.

✉ Piazza Campitelli 18 ☎ 06 686 4604 🕐 Closed Wed, 3 weeks Aug 🚌 To Via Arenula, Piazza Venezia

Bracciano
Trattoria del Castello (€€)
Classic, local cuisine, adapting medieval recipes to create special fish and meat dishes. Homemade pasta and an extensive wine list.

✉ Piazza Mazzini 1 ☎ 06 9980 4339 🕐 Closed Wed

Frascati
Cacciani (€€€)
Consistently reliable and spacious restaurant in the Castelli Romani with a large panoramic terrace from which to view Rome's urban conglomeration. Classic meat and fish dishes from Rome and Lazio. Try the regional white Frascati wine.

✉ Via A Diaz 15 ☎ 06 940 1991 🕐 Closed Mon

Zarazá (€–€€)
Simpler and cheaper than Cacciani featuring good traditional, regional fare.

✉ Via Viale Regina Margherita 45 ☎ 06 942 2053 🕐 Closed Mon, Sun dinner

Ostia Antica
Il Monumento (€€)
Simple, well-made fish and seafood dishes are the mainstay of this trattoria in the village near the ancient remains of Ostia. The house specialty, 'spaghetti monumento', is a wonderful mix of seafood and prawns.

✉ Piazza Umberto I 18 ☎ 06 565 0021 🕐 Closed Mon

Sperlonga
Agli Archi (€€€)
All the dishes at this little restaurant are delicious, from the antipasto of hot and cold seafood, to the homemade puddings. The menu changes daily to take advantage of that day's catches. Good-value wine list.

✉ Via Ottaviano 17 ☎ (0771) 548300 🕐 Closed Wed, except in Jul and Aug

Tivoli
Ristorante Antiche Terme di Diana (€€)
Well-established restaurant located in the attractive cellar of an old building. The pasta is freshly made on the premises and the menu has wholesome and traditional dishes.

✉ Via Sesii 6 ☎ (0774) 335239 🕐 Closed Mon

Villa Adriana
Adriano (€€–€€€)
One of the best options on the road to Villa Adriana where you can sit outside in the summer and enjoy a varied menu.

✉ Via di Villa Adriana 194 ☎ (0774) 382235 🕐 Closed Sun dinner

Viterbo
Richiastro (€)
Traditional local dishes that you will not find in many other places, using simple ingredients such as bread with a spread made from eggs and peppers, lentil and chick-pea soups, and tripe.

✉ Via della Marrocca 16–18 ☎ (0761) 228009 🕐 Closed Mon–Wed, Sun eve

What's in a Name?
In general, a trattoria is an unpretentious, family-run concern often with a regular clientele of local people who drop in when they do not want to cook for themselves. Ristoranti are usually more formal and expensive places for a special occasion. Osterie used to be the most basic of all, where simple dishes were washed down with jugs of local wine, but beware—recently the name has been adopted by some of the most expensive or touristy establishments.

Rome

Prices

Hotels in Rome are not cheap. The price brackets used here are for a double room—rooms in the mid and upper price ranges nearly always have private bathrooms. Those in the lower range do not always, but nearly all hotels will have at least a few rooms with private bathrooms.

€   = up to €100
€€ = €100–€200
€€€ = more than€200

Campo dei Fiori (€€)

Situated in one of the loveliest quarters of central Rome, this hotel (terrace overlooks Roman rooftops) is in a flaking ochre-coloured street. Pleasant decor and multi-lingual staff.

✉ Via del Biscione 6 ☎ 06 688 06865, fax 687 6003; www.hotelcampdefiori.com
🚊 To Corso Vittorio, Largo Argentina

Campo Marzio (€)

If you want a no-frills place to rest your head then this low-cost family-run *pensione*, although a little drab, is clean and superbly situated two steps from parliament and the Pantheon.

✉ Piazza Campo Marzio 7 ☎ 06 688 01486 🚊 To Largo di Torre Argentina

Canova (€€€)

Refurbished in the summer of 1996 this 3-star, comfortably appointed hotel is in a lovely, quiet and safe street near the station at Santa Maria Maggiore.

✉ Via Urbana 10/a ☎ 06 487 3314, fax 06 481 9123; www.canovahotelroma.it
🚇 Cavour 🚊 To Via Cavour

Caravaggio (€€)

The lovely wooden-framed door gives the impression of a private club and the atmosphere of this refurbished, centrally located hotel is as welcoming as you might expect.

✉ Via Palermo 73 ☎ 06 485 915, fax 06 474 7363
🚇 Repubblica 🚊 To Via Nazionale

Della Conciliazione (€€)

Situated in one of the lovely streets tucked away behind the Vatican. The rooms are a little small but they are pleasantly furnished. Friendly service from a multi-lingual staff.

✉ Via Borgo Pio 163/166 ☎ 06 686 7910, fax 06 6880 1164
🚊 To Piazza del Risorgimento

Coppedè (€€)

A refurbished small establishment a little out of the central district in the much sought-after residential area designed by the weird and wonderful architect from which the hotel takes its name. Excellent value for price category.

✉ Via Chiana 88 ☎ 06 854 9535, fax 06 854 2261; www.hotelcoppede.com
🚊 To Via Po

Corot (€€)

Right next to the station so perfectly placed for getting to all sights both in and out of town, this hotel offers comfortable rooms and a hospitable and multi-lingual staff.

✉ Via Marghera 15/17 ☎ 06 4470 0900, fax 06 4470 0905; www.hotelcorot.it 🚇 Termini
🚊 To Termini

Cosmopolita (€€)

Large, marble-floored rooms, courteous English and French-speaking staff, located right in the heart of town (so ask for inward-facing rooms). All facilities. Buffet breakfast included.

✉ Via Santa Eufemia 5 ☎ 06 6994 1349; fax 06 6994 1360; www.hotelcosmopolita.com
🚊 To Piazza Venezia

D'Inghilterra (€€€)

A very classy place, situated in a most elegant area of the city. Over a century old it

boasts former guests such as Hemingway and Liszt.
✉ Via Bocca di Leone 14
☎ 06 699811, fax 06 6992 2243;
www.royaldemeure.com
🚌 To Piazza San Silvestro

Elite (€€)
A moderately priced, very comfortable small hotel in an expensive area. It also has air-conditioning, an important consideration in central Rome in the summer.
✉ Via F. Crispi 49 ☎ 06 678 3083, fax 06 679 1761 🚇 Barberini 🚌 To Via del Tritone

Emmaus (€€)
This fourth-floor 28-roomed hotel (some of the rooms have a view of St. Peter's dome) is excellent value for this category. It has satellite TV and, unusually, wheelchair access.
✉ Via delle Fornaci 23 ☎ 06 635 658; www.emmaushotel.com 🚌 To Via Gregorio VII

Enrica (€)
This inexpensive hotel near Rome's student quarter is run by a friendly multi-lingual ex-sailor and his wife. It has its own lovely garden.
✉ Viale Castro Pretorio 25
☎ 06 445 3742 🚇 Castro Pretorio 🚌 To Via Castro Pretorio

Esquilino (€€)
On the 'clean' side of the station, this lovingly refurbished hotel is run by two professional hoteliers. Some rooms look out at Santa Maria Maggiore but the courtyard is quieter.
✉ Piazza dell'Esquilino 29
☎ 06 474 3454, fax 06 474 1570 🚇 Termini 🚌 To Piazza dell'Esquilino

Excelsior, Westin (€€€)
Probably the most prestigious hotel in Rome with a luxury and service reminiscent of the days before mass travel.

✉ Via Vittorio Veneto 125
☎ 06 47081, fax 06 482 6205;
www.westin.com/excelsior rome 🚇 Barberini 🚌 To Vittorio Veneto

Firenze (€€)
Completely restored at the end of 1995, on the first floor of a chic but busy street (near the Spanish Steps) so get a courtyard room.
✉ Via Due Macelli 106 ☎ 06 679 7240, fax 06 678 5636;
www.hotelfirenzeroma.it
🚇 Barberini 🚌 To Via del Tritone

Hassler–Villa Medici (€€€)
One of the grandest old-style luxury hotels in the heart of the most elegant part of the city with a view to die for from the elegant roof terrace.
✉ Piazza Trinità dei Monti 6
☎ 06 699340, fax 06 678999;
www.hotelhasslerroma.com
🚇 Spagna 🚌 To Via del Tritone

In Parione Piccolo (€€)
In a great location in the old city close to Campo de'Fiori, this 16-room hotel has been remodelled. Roof garden.
✉ Via Chiavari 32 ☎ 06 6880 2560, fax 06 683 4094;
www.inparione.com 🚌 To Corso Vittorio Emanuele

Ludovisi Palace (€€€)
Smart hotel renovated from a 1920s townhouse near the Via Veneto. Bright and fresh with excellent service.
✉ Via Ludovisi 43 ☎ 06 4202 0396/4202 0741; www.ludovisi palacehotel.com 🚇 Spagna/Barberini 🚌 To Via Veneto

Madrid (€€)
At the top end of the moderate-price category, this 26-roomed hotel has all the amenities and a delightful inside courtyard-terrace.
✉ Via Mario de' Fiori 93/5
☎ 06 699 1510, fax 06 679 1653;
www.hotelmadridroma.com
🚌 To Piazza San Silvestro

Reservations
There are some 700 hotels in Rome but reserving early is still advisable. Even the most modest places may want a telephone booking backed up by a deposit (a credit card will usually, but not always, be enough). If you do reserve, the local EPT tourist offices will help. There is an office in the centre (Via Parigi 11; ☎ 06 3600 4399/06 488 991) and at the station (☎ 06 4890 6300) with multi-lingual staff.

Rome & Excursions from the City

Special Needs

Italian culture and society may not accommodate special requirements formally, but the flexibility and initiative of the people means you could encounter extraordinary gestures of generosity (alternatively, you may find your path irremediably blocked). For example, hotels with no night porter often provide a key for guests who want to stay out late; those without breakfast may miraculously produce coffee. Unfortunately, the nature of Roman building does not lend itself to wheelchairs, but, whatever the official line, check with the individual establishment first.

Navona (€)

For a one-star rated hotel Navona is a find. Only one minute from the Piazza Navona and most of the 15 rooms have been renovated to a good standard. Best to take breakfast at a nearby bar. You will need to reserve well in advance.
✉ Via dei Sediari 8 ☎ 06 686 4203, fax 06 6880 3802; www.hotelnavona.com 🚌 To Corso del Rinascimento

Perugia (€)

Modest with no frills, but with a friendly multi-lingual staff and most of the 13 rooms have bathrooms. Two steps from the Colosseum.
✉ Via del Colosseo 7 ☎ 06 679 7200, fax 06 678 4635; www.hperugia.it 🚇 Colosseo 🚌 To Via Cavour, Colosseo

Ponte Sisto (€€€)

An enormous hotel for the area (103 rooms). It offers all the basic amenities and a terrace in a beautiful part of the historical heart of town.
✉ Via dei Pettinari 64 ☎ 06 686310, fax 06 6830 1712; www. hotelpontesisto.it 🚌 To Via Arenula

Portoghesi (€€)

Tucked away in a lovely side street in one of the prettiest areas. Tastefully furnished, with a roof terrace.
✉ Via dei Portoghesi 1 ☎ 06 686 4231, fax 06 687 6976; www.hotelportoghesiroma.com 🚌 To Corso del Rinascimento

La Residenza (€€)

Well-placed near Via Vittorio Veneto and Villa Borghese, this hotel evokes the atmosphere of an elegant private house. Stylish, spacious rooms plus a terrace and roof garden.
✉ Via Emilia 22/4 ☎ 06 488 0789, fax 06 485721; www. giannettihotelsgroup.com 🚇 Barberini 🚌 To Via Vittorio Veneto

Ripa (€€€)

Space and light is optimized at this Trastevere hotel in a minimalist style. Popular with visiting Italians.
✉ Via Luigi Giannitti 21 ☎ 06 586611, fax 06 586 1832; www.ripahotel.com 🚌 To Viale Trastevere

San Paolo (€)

Basic but clean and bright on a lovely street, with friendly staff. Twenty two rooms (many with own bathroom). Group discounts available.
✉ Via Panisperna 95 ☎ 06 474 5213, fax 06 474 5218; www.hotelsanpaoloroma.com 🚇 Cavour 🚌 To Via Cavour

Sant'Anselmo (€€)

A lovely reasonably priced hotel in a villa with garden in the heart of ancient Rome; wheelchair facilities.
✉ Piazza Sant'Anselmo 2 ☎ 06 574 5174, fax 06 578 3604 🚇 Circo Massimo 🚌 To Via Aventino

Shangri la' Corsetti (€€)

Situated out of the central district beyond EUR, with every amenity including a good restaurant.
✉ Viale Algeria 141 ☎ 06 591 6441, fax 06 541 3813; www. shangrilacorsetti.it 🚇 EUR Fermi 🚌 To Palazzo dello Sporto

Smeraldo (€€)

An excellent location just a few minutes' walk from the Campo de'Fiori. Upgraded to three-stars, the 50 rooms are now improved and all the bathrooms are new.

✉ **Vicolo dei Chiodaroli 9** ☎ **06 687 5929, fax 06 6880 5495; www.smeraldoroma.com** 🚌 **To Corso Vittorio Emanuele II, Largo di Torre Argentina**

Sole al Pantheon (€€€)

With some rooms looking over the Pantheon, this hotel has had some illustrious guests not least Ariosto, one of Italian literature's greats.

✉ **Piazza della Rotunda 63** ☎ **06 678 0441; www.hotel solealpantheon.com** 🚌 **To Largo di Torre Argentina**

Della Torre Argentina (€€)

Friendly well-run hotel where old gracefully blends with modern. The bedrooms are large and well equipped. Roof terrace.

✉ **Corso Vittorio Emanuele 102** ☎ **06 683 3886, fax 06 6880 1641; www.dellatorreargentina. com** 🚌 **Corso Vittorio Emanuele**

Youth Hostels
YWCA (€)

The safe women-only hostel near the central station is the perfect option if you are in Rome for early starts and serious sightseeing. There is an evening curfew.

✉ **Via Cesare Balbo 4** ☎ **06 488 0460** 🚇 **Termini** 🚌 **To Via Cavour**

Ostelli de la Gioventù Foro Italico (€)

Members of the Youth Hostel Association can use this Youth Hostel a little way from central Rome. Bed-and-breakfast, half and full board.

✉ **Viale delle Olimpiadi 61** ☎ **06 323 6267; www. ostellionline.org** 🚌 **To Viale delle Olimpiadi**

Campsites
Parco del Lago (€)

A tranquil campsite set on the edge of Lake Bracciano. All necessary amenities, and popular with Romans who come to get away from it all. Reserve early. Available in summer only.

✉ **Lungolago di Polline 75, Strada Provinciale Anguillara–Trevignano Km 4,100** ☎ **06 9980 2003; www.parcodellago. com** 🚌 **To Anguillara/ Trevignano**

Flaminio Village (€)

A large and reasonably priced campsite within reach of the city, offering cabins among its options. There is a swimming pool. Open March to December.

✉ **Via Flaminia Nuova Km 8,200** ☎ **06 333 2604; www.flaminio.com** 🚌 **Bus or train to Due Ponti**

Castelfusano Country Club (€)

This is one of the two campsites near the not-so-clean but long and wide Roman beaches. Rome is easily reached by public transportation. Open all year.

✉ **Piazza di Castelfusano 1, Ostia** ☎ **06 5618 5490/1; www. countryclubcastelfusano.it** 🚇 **To Castelfusano**

La Torraccia
Hotel la Torraccia (€€)

An option which is not-too-distant from Rome and near the Etruscan ruins. Every room has a terrace.

✉ **Viale Mediterraneo 45, Tarquinia Lido** ☎ **(0766) 864 375/8642; www.torraccia.it** 🚇 **To Tarquinia**

Tivoli
Delle Terme (€€)

This 3-star hotel with its own gardens and restaurant, conveniently placed for the villas of Tivoli, is a fine alternative to staying centrally, not least because the price goes down by half for the privilege of being in a small attractive countryside town.

✉ **Piazza B della Quiete 5** ☎ **(0774) 371033** 🚇 **To Tivoli**

The Cost of a Star

The Italian star-rating system can make it difficult to know what you are getting, as it is based exclusively on facilities offered. This means, for example, a charmingly furnished atmospheric 2-star affair may cost less than a grotty run-down 3-star business. This is further complicated by a fewer-stars-less-tax situation with some hoteliers happy not to upgrade themselves.

Antiques, Art, Books Toys & Fashion

Where to Find Antiques

If you are looking for antiques (from an old print of Rome to furniture) the most prestigious shops are on Via del Babuino. Another safe and reliable destination is Via Guilia. At the end of May and October, just before and after the blistering heat, Via dei Coronari, which has only antiques, holds its fair. The shops open late, the street is carpeted red and lined with candles. It is a magical atmosphere, perfect for a evening stroll.

Antiques

Antichità
Located in an area with some interesting antique shops, albeit pricey, Antichità specializes in old fabrics and furnishings.
✉ Via del Babuino 83
☎ 06 320 7585 🚇 Spagna
🚌 To Piazzale Flaminio

Art Import
A slightly unprepossessing name but a treasure trove if you are after antique silver. They also stock porcelain, an interesting collection of *objéts d'art* and modern Italian Barbini glass vases.
✉ Via del Babuino 150
☎ 06 3600 2178 🚇 Spagna
🚌 To Piazzale Flaminio

La Sinopia
On a street with several antique shops, you will find objects of high quality and although prices are high they do offer value for money.
✉ Via dei Banchi Vecchi 21c
☎ 06 687 2869 🚌 To Corso Vittorio Emanuele II

Art

Alberto di Castro
Definitely the shop to visit for authentic prints. It stretches far back off the street and is lined with prints of all price ranges. A great selection of framed or unframed Roman scenes.
✉ Via del Babuino 71 ☎ 06 361 3752 🚇 Spagna 🚌 To Piazza San Silvestro, Via del Tritone

Maria Grazia Luffarelli
Specializes in watercolours, especially land and seascapes. Also a range of Roman watercolour reproductions in postcard form. Prices range from very low to moderate for orginal works by the artist.
✉ Via dei Banchi Vecchi 29
☎ 06 683 2494 🚌 To Corso Vittorio Emanuele II

Books

Almost Corner Bookshop
This small but well-stocked English bookshop in Trastevere offers a good selection of classic and recent fiction and non-fiction, as well as a wide range of books on Italy.
✉ Via del Moro 45 ☎ 06 583 6942 🚌 To Piazza Sonnino

Bookshop Electa
Museum bookshop on Capitoline Hill. Reasonable prices for museum guides, mythological and historical literature plus artefacts and artwork.
✉ Piazza del Campidoglio
☎ 06 3996 7800 🚌 To Piazza Venezia

Feltrinelli
The best-stocked bookshop chain in Rome. Conveniently located branches and easy-to-understand merchandising. Also cards, specialist magazines, posters, videos and CD-Roms.
✉ Largo di Torre Argentina 5a
☎ 06 6880 3248 🚌 To Largo di Torre Argentina

Mel Bookshop
One of the largest, newest bookshops in Rome. 'Mel' has a good English section. It sells everything from kids' books to CDs and even has a café in the art department.
✉ Via Nazionale 254/5 ☎ 06 488 5405 🚇 Repubblica
🚌 To Via Nazionale

Touring Viaggi

This bookshop and travel agent of the Touring Club Italiano stocks all you need in terms of maps and guides as well as a small selection of tasteful postcards.

✉ **Via del Babuino 20**
☎ **06 3600 5281** 🚇 **Spagna, Flaminio** 🚌 **To Piazzale Flaminio**

Children's Clothes and Toys

Bortolucci

A wonderful model car takes centre stage among this array of pine-wood toys beautifully crafted and designed by members of the Bortolucci family.

✉ **Via dei Pastini 98** ☎ **06 6919 0894** 🚌 **To Piazza della Rotonda**

La Cicogna

Chic high-quality Italian kids' fashion and elegantly practical maternity clothes, well-made but at somewhat high prices. You can get some great bargains if you catch the sales. There are several outlets in the city.

✉ **Via Frattina 138** ☎ **06 679 1912** 🚌 **To Via del Corso**

Città del Sole

An inspired selection of top-of-the-range educational toys and books for children of all ages. The shop adopts a pretty hands-on, child-friendly approach.

✉ **Via della Scrofa 65**
☎ **06 6880 3805** 🚌 **To Corso del Rinascimento**

Invicta

No self-respecting Italian schoolkid can be seen without an 'Invicta' knapsack, so established that it is now officially part of the Italian language.

✉ **Via del Babuino 27/8**
☎ **06 3600 1737** 🚇 **Spagna** 🚌 **To Piazzale Flaminio, Piazza San Silvestro**

Al Sogno

Sogno means dream but this shop could be a parent's nightmare given the prices of the wonderful stock, which sometimes resembles museum pieces. Particularly tempting are the soft toys.

✉ **Piazza Navona 53**
☎ **06 686 4198** 🚌 **To Corso del Rinascimento**

Fashion: designer

Arsenale

Located just off Piazza Navona, owner Patrizia Pieroni's outlet showcases her own romantic designs. An interesting mix between classic and original, and they incorporate the most wonderful velvets, silks, linens and lace.

✉ **Via del Governo Vecchio 64**
☎ **06 686 1380** 🚌 **To Corso Vittorio Emanuele**

Brioni

Located close to the famous Via Vittorio Veneto, Brioni has been dressing royalty and celebrities since 1945 and is regarded as one of Italy's top tailors. The suits and tuxedos reflect the highest standards of quality and craftsmanship. This, the largest store, also has ready-to-wear for both men and women. Other branches on Via Condotti and Via Vittorio Veneto.

✉ **Via Barberini** ☎ **06 484517** 🚇 **Barberini** 🚌 **To Via Barberini**

Davide Cenci

High quality, classic and classy. Davide Cenci is synonymous in Rome with low-key tailored elegance and is as refined as an old-style English outfitters. The prices are to match. You'll find Burberry, Church's, Ralph Lauren and more.

✉ **Via Campo Marzio 1/7**
☎ **06 699 0681** 🚌 **To Largo di Torre Argentina, Via del Corso**

Opening and Closing

Shop opening hours are beginning to change with more all-day and Sunday openings and the traditional August shut-down is weakening as Romans begin to take shorter holidays.
Generally, however, it is a Monday to Saturday set-up with a break from 1pm to 4pm. Food shops often close on Thursday afternoons and others on Monday mornings.

Fashion, Interiors, Jewellery, & Leather

Prices
Prices in Rome are not low, a state of affairs that is not helped by the preponderance of small shops, which has made for an inefficient retailing system. The tradition is hard to kill. Italian life is public and the local shop, particularly the foodstore, is a place to chat, have things put aside for you, receive discounts and even credit. As a visitor you can expect to be excluded.

VAT Refunds
Non-EU citizens spending more than €155 are entitled to VAT refunds, so be sure to buy from those shops displaying the sticker. You will be furnished with a form to present to customs on leaving Italy along with the *scontrino* (receipt). Do not use or wear the goods first.

Giorgio Armani
The beautifully cut, hand-finished simplicity of the Milanese designer resides in the prestigious Via Condotti. Look for the slightly less expensive off-the-peg *Emporio* line, which is round the corner on Via del Babuino.
✉ Via Condotti 77 ☎ 06 699 1460 Ⓜ Spagna 🚌 To Via del Corso

Fendi
There are fur coats, shoes and ready-to-wear clothes, but it is the much-copied signature handbag with the discreet 'F' in the design that is the classic purchase for both Romans and visitors.
✉ Via Borgognona 36/40 ☎ 06 679 7641 Ⓜ Spagna 🚌 To Piazza Augusto Imperatore

Gucci
Another classic Italian fashion-house offers inimitable wares in a soothing creamy-beige outlet on the most chic street in Rome.
✉ Via Condotti 8 ☎ 06 679 0405 Ⓜ Spagna 🚌 To Via del Corso

Missoni
The multi-hued elegance of the inspired tapestry-like knitwear is almost outrageous. The beach towels offer a taste of the style, if you can not stretch to a sweater.
✉ Piazza di Spagna 78 ☎ 06 679 2555 Ⓜ Spagna 🚌 To Via del Corso

Max Mara
The affordable end of designer land, Max Mara offers wonderfully crisp shapes and clean tones in various branches.
✉ Via Condotti 46a ☎ 06 6992 2104 Ⓜ Spagna 🚌 To Via del Corso

Prada
Prestigious Italian fashion label based in Milan. Men and women's clothes, shoes and accessories.
✉ Via del Babuino 91 ☎ 06 3600 4884 Ⓜ Spagna 🚌 To Piazza di Spagna

Roberto Cavalli
A chic boutique owned by Italian fashion mogul Roberto Cavalli. Elegant designs in his own unique style.
✉ Piazza di Spagna ☎ 06 679 2294 Ⓜ Spagna 🚌 To Piazza di Spagna

Valentino
Rome's own has his boutique on Via Condotti just two steps from the wonderful headquarters in Piazza Mignatelli. The casual wear 'Oliver' is round the corner on Via del Babuino.
✉ Via Condotti 13 ☎ 06 6789 5862 Ⓜ Spagna 🚌 To Via del Corso

Fashion: 'non-label'

Gente
One of the best women's clothes shops in Rome, on the city's most popular shopping street. 'Gente' sells lots of wearable styles (including many designer labels). Other branches in the central area.
✉ Via Cola di Renzo 277 ☎ 06 321 1516 🚌 To Piazza Cavour

Lei
For good quality, fairly pricey but seriously wearable young

adult fashions go here. Among others they stock the smart, simple French label Tara. Some shoes and accessories.

✉ **Via Nazionale 88** ☎ **06 482 1700** 🚌 **To Via Nazionale**

Pinko

Trendy up-to-the-minute fashions for women in their twenties and thirties.

✉ **Via Due Macelli 91/95** ☎ **06 6920 2091** 🚌 **To Via dei Tritone**

Interior Design

Bagagli

A veritable field-day is to be had in this cobblestoned shop if you want tableware. Villeroy and Boch and the wonderful Alessi designs, which are among the best-quality ranges on offer.

✉ **Via di Campo Marzio 42** ☎ **06 687 1406** 🚌 **To Via del Corso**

Frette

The queen of household linens. The bed linen and towels, often inspired by classical designs, are quite beautiful, as are the prices unless your trip happens to coincide with the sales.

✉ **Via Nazionale 80** ☎ **06 488 2641** 🚌 **To Via Nazionale**

Modigliani

Four levels make up this interesting store on Via Condotti. Modigliani creates ceramics, tableware and Murano glass objects for decoration and the table. Climb the crystal staircase while you are there.

✉ **Via Condotti 24** ☎ **06 678 5653** Ⓜ **Spagna** 🚌 **To Via del Corso**

Spazio Sette

By no means cheap but quite easily the best home shop in town selling everything from glassware to hardware, postcards to furniture. The

buying philosophy seems to be 'If it is designer...'.

✉ **Via dei Barbieri 7** ☎ **06 6880 4261** 🚌 **To Largo di Torre Argentina**

Jewellery

Barbara Spinelli

This Italian goldsmith creates exquisite modern designs using precious and semi-precious stones such as amber.

✉ **Via dei Prefetti 25** ☎ **06 6830 1131** 🚌 **To Via del Corso**

Bulgari

While France has Cartier, Italy has Bulgari. Classic yet modern designs in the very best of materials including diamonds, pearls and gold. Also elegant watches.

✉ **Via Condotti 10** ☎ **06 696261** Ⓜ **Spagna** 🚌 **To Via del Corso**

Raggi

A fine shop for its wide selection at reasonable prices, with several branches in the city. This branch is on one of the best shopping streets in Rome.

✉ **Via Cola di Rienzo 250** ☎ **06 689 6601** 🚌 **To Piazza Cavour**

Leather

Catello D'Auria

A lovely little drawer-lined shop with a small but excellent selection of leather gloves; they also sell hosiery.

✉ **Via Due Macelli 55** ☎ **06 679 3364** Ⓜ **Spagna** 🚌 **To Via del Tritone**

Red and Blue

An excellent place to go if you are looking for top-quality leatherwear in the classic styles reflected by its other merchandise, (for example Burberry).

✉ **Via due Macelli 57/8** ☎ **06 679 1933** Ⓜ **Spagna** 🚌 **To Via del Tritone**

Department Stores

Department stores are not the Italian style. If they are yours, the less touristy Piazza Fiume (not far from Via Veneto) is the best bet. Here you will find the larger of the Rinascente (the other is on Via del Corso) with kitchenware, furnishings and a café and, nearby, the old Peroni beer factory has been lovingly converted into Coin.

Accessories, Shoes, Stationery, Souvenirs & Markets

Souvenir Shopping

Characteristic Roman souvenirs consist of copies of the main sights or bronze reproductions of Etruscan objects, all of which can be found in most tobacconists at half the price of the stalls near the sights themselves. Ecclesiastical memorabilia is to be had in the shops in and around Borgo Pio, while shops supplying the religious community are on Via dei Cestari near the Pantheon.

Accessories

Borsalino

An old-fashioned hat shop that is the most famous in Rome for its classic men's headwear and more changeable women's styles.

✉ **Piazza del Popolo 20** ☎ **06 323 3353** 🚇 **Flaminio** 🚌 **To Piazza Popolo**

Marissa Padovani

The ultimate place to buy swimming costumes—as well as a good range of ready-to-wear, you can have your bikini or one-piece made to measure. Sometimes you can be lucky to find some items in the sale.

✉ **Via delle Carrozze 81** ☎ **06 679 3946** 🚇 **Spagna** 🚌 **To Via del Corso**

Mondello Ottica

Rome is full of opticians and designer glasses shops, Mondello is a bit different. Prices are a little higher than average, but the frames are the hippest and the quality superb. Any problems with broken glasses while in Rome this is the place to get that repair done.

✉ **Via del Pellegrino 98** ☎ **06 686 1955** 🚌 **To Corso Vittorio Emanuele II**

Stationery

Antoca Cartotecnica

In business since 1930 this is a pen-lover's heaven. A wide array of modern and vintage fountain pens, antique steel nibs, ink and old stationery. All is beautfully displayed. Not far from the Pantheon.

✉ **Piazza dei Caprettari 61** ☎ **06 687 5671** 🚌 **To Largo di Torre Argentina**

Campo Marzio Penne

Specializes in antique, calligraphic and major-brand pens (and restoration). The new Vatican collection pen is based on designs by Raphael in the Vatican museums.

✉ **Campo Marzio 41** ☎ **06 6880 7877** 🚌 **To Via del Corso**

Pantheon

A gorgeous little shop which sells hand-marbled paper, notebooks and photo albums as well as a great selection of writing paper and cards.

✉ **Via della Rotonda 15** ☎ **06 687 5313** 🚌 **To Largo di Torre Argentina**

Vertecchi

A serious and modern stationery shop selling an excellent selection of pens, writing paper (also by the sheet in a variety of shades). There is a large artist's section.

✉ **Via della Croce 70** ☎ **06 670 0155** 🚇 **Flaminio** 🚌 **To Via del Corso**

Shoes

Dominici

A pristine white-tiled shop in which this Roman designer's original shoes are displayed in neat rows. The prices are good and the styles a bit out of the ordinary without being over the top.

✉ **Via del Corso 14** ☎ **06 361 0591** 🚌 **To Via del Corso**

Impronta

A small shop but with a good collection of young fashion styles. It is on the piazza at the beginning of this atmospheric shopping street.

✉ **Via del Governo Vecchio 1** ☎ **06 689 6947** 🚌 **To Corso Vittorio Emmanuele**

Bruno Magli

These incredibly elegant, classic Italian shoes for ladies and gentlemen can be found near the other classic Italian fashion shops.

✉ Via del Gambero 1 ☎ 06 679 3802 🚍 To Piazza San Silvestro

Lattanzi

Exclusive hand-crafted shoes in the finest leather made lovingly in the most traditional of methods. Recognized world-wide for their durability and elegance.

✉ Via Bocca di Leone 59 ☎ 06 678 6119 🚇 Spagna 🚍 To Via del Corso

Ramirez

Part of a chain and thus competitively priced; boasts a wide selection of shoe styles for both sexes as well as all age groups.

✉ Via Frattina 85/a ☎ 06 679 2467 🚇 Spagna 🚍 To Via del Corso

Fausto Santini

The ultimate in modern Roman shoe design, Fausto Santini's styles are original and elegant with nothing quite like them elsewhere.

✉ Via Frattina 120/21 ☎ 06 678 4114 🚇 Spagna 🚍 To Via del Corso

Souvenirs and Religious Gifts

Galleria Savelli

Founded by Lorenzo Savelli in 1898 the family still produce religious artefacts close to St. Peter's. There is also a new showroom for mosaics in Via Paolo.

✉ Piazza Pio XII 1/2 ☎ 06 6880 6383 🚍 To Piazza del Risorgimento

Soprani

One of the many shops around the Vatican dedicated to serious religious objects and more commercially minded souvenirs of your trip to the Holy City; images of the Pope and Christ can be printed on almost everything.

✉ Via del Mascherino 29 ☎ 06 6880 1404 🚍 To Piazza del Risorgimento

Markets

Campo de' Fiori

Probably the loveliest food market in central Rome thanks to the wonderful piazza hosting it. Open every morning except Sundays, the wall of flower-sellers can be found all day.

✉ Piazza Campo dei Fiori 🚍 To Corso Vittorio

Vittorio Emmanuele

The largest food market in Rome, also the cheapest, has often been criticized for lowering the tone of this splendid piazza. But it is now under cover in the vast former barracks of Ex-Caserma Sani nearby. There is a wonderful array of fish and fruit and vegetables.

✉ Ex-Caserma Sani di Piazza Vittoria 🚇 Vittorio 🚍 To Piazza Vittorio Emmanuele

Porta Portese

This market is famous throughout Italy. It takes over the streets in and around Porta Portese every Sunday morning and is jam-packed. You can buy almost everything imaginable from clothes (beware of fake labels) to books and antiques.

✉ Via Porta Portese 🚍 To Viale Trastevere

Via Sannio

Popular with Romans for new and second-hand clothes. The leather jackets are excellent value and the shoe stands are good. Some real bargains in the piles at the back if you have an eye.

✉ Via Sannio 🚇 San Giovanni 🚍 To Via Appia Nuova

Food Shopping

Supermarket shopping is not so popular in Italy as it is in other European countries and much shopping for food and everyday goods is still done in tiny local shops known as *alimentari*. These general stores sell everything from olive oil and pasta to basic household needs. They usually have a delicatessen counter, where you can have a sandwich made up from the meats and cheeses that are on display. Dotted throughout the city are some wonderful delis selling an astounding variety of breads, cheeses, hams, fresh pasta and even ready-made dishes.

Ancient Sights, Museums & Theme Parks

Christmas
From the beginning of December until Epiphany (6 January) Rome is decorated with delicate street lighting and, on some streets, red carpets. Piazza Navona is taken over by a massive Christmas market selling an exotic range of gaudy sweets, cheap toys and Christmas decorations. In addition many churches have *presepi* (nativity scenes), often with valuable old models placed in realistic Renaissance street scenes.

Ancient Sights
To help get to grips with ancient Rome, the souvenir stands outside the major sights sell little books that show many of the ancient remains as they are now and as they were when they were intact. The gaudy souvenirs on sale here should also appeal to children.

Colosseo (Colosseum)
See the corridors through which lions came on their way to eat Christians. (► 18).

Largo Argentina
Full of serene cats and the remains of a massive public lavatory (► 45).

Museo della Civiltà Romana
Models of what ancient Rome was really like (► 48).

Ostia Antica
Well-preserved remains of an ancient Roman seaside town (► 86).

Via Appia Antica
The road ancient Romans travelled on their way to the sea, west to Ostia, east to the other side of Italy (► 62).

Churches

San Clemente
Underneath this pretty mosaic-filled church are secret corridors leading to ancient remains (► 23).

Sant'Ignazio di Loyola
Here you really can see up to heaven by looking at the magnificent *trompe l'oeil* ceiling (► 66).

Santa Maria della Concezione
The macabre crypt is decorated with the bones of defunct monks (► 68).

Santa Maria in Cosmedin
Put your hand into the mouth of truth, which was originally an ancient Roman drain cover and probably represented the sun (► 68).

The Catacombs
Definitely not for the faint-hearted child—these kilometres-long underground passages are lined with the tombs of early Christians (► 38).

Museums

Castel Sant'Angelo
This tomb-come-fortress-come-palace has some wonderful *trompe l'oeils* and lots of winding, secret corridors, gloomy guardrooms and good views (► 17).

Explora, il Museo dei Bambini
Explora is the first museum in Rome especially aimed at children—the under 12s. Here they are allowed to touch and play with a range of educational exhibits. Hands-on is the key here.
✉ Via Flaminia 82 ☎ 06 361 3766, www.mdbr.it ⓘ Tue–Sat 9–6.45, Sun 10–6.45
🚇 To Via Flaminia

Galleria Spada
Visit the Galleria in Palazzo Spada particularly for its spectacular three-dimensional *trompe l'oeil*, whose fake perspective will make even the smallest child seem tall (► 56).

Museo delle Cere

The surreality of some of the tableaux may appeal more to adult senses of humour than to children used to Madame Tussaud's, but it is still worth going to see what Leonardo and his contemporaries might have looked like. Around 250 famous personalities in wax.

✉ Piazza dei Santi Apostoli 67 ☎ 06 679 6482; www. museodellacere.it ⏰ 9–8 🚌 To Piazza Venezia

Museo di Roma in Trastevere

As well as paintings of what Rome looked like when all these artists were strolling around, there are some amusing waxworks of Roman and rustic life in the 18th century (► 48).

Outdoor: Parks and Shows

Aquafelix

A water park with an exotic range of themed rides and slides involving getting wet and screaming—most children under five may find it a little too much. There are also shops, a bar and a self-service restaurant.

✉ Autostrada Roma– Civitavecchia at the Civitavecchia Nord Exit ☎ (0766) 32221 ⏰ Jun–Sep, 10–6 daily

Aquapiper

An outdoor swimming pool complex with a children's pool complete with a slide, another pool with a wave machine and its own more exciting (or terrifying, depending on your point of view) slide. Also ponies and camels, a picnic area, a bar and a games room.

✉ Via Maremmana Inferiore Km 29, Guidonia ☎ (0774) 326 538 ⏰ First week Jun to first week Sep daily 9–7 🚌 From Ponte Mammolo to Palombara

Bioparco

Rome's zoo underwent a transformation in the late 1990s to re-emerge as a champion of environmental awareness. In place of the old museum mentality, visitors are encouraged to learn more about the natural habitats of the animals and to play an active part in their conservation.

✉ Piazzale del Giardino Zoologico, Villa Borghese ☎ 06 360 8211 ⏰ Apr–end Oct 9.30–6 (Sat, Sun and hols 9.30–7 early Apr–late Sep); Nov–end Mar Mon–Fri 9.30–5 🚌 To Piazza Ungheria

Piazza Navona

There is always plenty to see here; you can pose for a portrait or caricature, buy a helium-filled balloon, eat ice-cream or people watch. There is Bernini's wonderful fountain to set your imagination flying (► 21).

Luna Park (Luneur)

This 30-year-old funfair is the nearest that Rome gets to a theme park. Most of its attractions are fairly traditional—a hall of mirrors, a ferris wheel, roller-coasters and merry-go-rounds—but recent additions include some more ambitious contraptions and stage-sets based on American theme-park rides.

✉ Via delle Tre Fontane ☎ 592 5933; www.luneur.it ⏰ Telephone for latest opening details 🚇 Magliana 🚌 To Via delle Tre Fontane

Carnevale

Carnevale takes place the week before Shrove Tuesday and children dress up as cartoon or historical characters, animals and so on to walk through the streets with their parents, letting off fire crackers and throwing confetti.

Cinema, Theatre, Live Music

Hollywood on the Tiber

Rome has had an active film industry since 1937 when Mussolini opened the studios at Cinecittà. The heyday of 'Hollywood on the Tiber' was in the 1950s and 1960s when many American producers and directors came here to make films such as *Ben Hur*, *Cleopatra* and, of course, the famous spaghetti westerns.

Cinema

Italy is proud of its high standard of dubbing and most foreign films are dubbed into Italian. Cinema screenings are usually at 4.30, 6.30, 8.30 and 10.30. In the summer (June to September), there are several open-air cinemas, showing mainly classics or the previous season's most successful releases.

L'Alcazar

One of the first to show the recent releases, this cinema is located in the Trastevere district. Films shown in English or with English sub-titles on Mondays.

✉ Via Cardinal Merry del Val 14 ☎ 06 588 0099 🚋 To Viale Trastevere, Piazza Sonnino

Metropolitan

Modern multiplex showing all the latest blockbusters.

✉ Via del Corso 7 ☎ 06 320 0933 Ⓜ Flaminio 🚋 To Via del Corso

Nuovo Sacher

This cinema belongs to film-maker Nanni Moretti (of *Caro Diario* fame) and is named after his favourite cake. It shows slightly offbeat new releases (which appeal to the proprietor) and screens them in original language (which can be anything) on Mondays and Tuesdays. There is an outdoor arena where films are shown during the summer.

✉ Largo Ascianghi 1 ☎ 06 581 8116 🚋 To Viale Trastevere

Pasquino

Overhauled and updated the Pasquino is the first English language cinema in Rome. The two cinemas show English-language films only (usually with Italian sub-titles).

✉ Vicolo del Piede 19 ☎ 06 580 3622 🚋 To Viale Trastevere, Piazza Sonnino

Warner Village Moderno

Five large screens in this utra-modern complex—new releases in English every Thursday. Great sound and comfy seats.

✉ Piazza della Repubblica 45/6 ☎ 06 4777 9209 Ⓜ Repubblica 🚋 To Piazza della Repubblica

Theatre and Dance

Argentina

A beautiful, restored 19th-century gem that occasionally hosts TV spectaculars. Home to the Rome Theatre Company, who do good (if slightly traditional) productions of ancient and modern classics.

✉ Largo di Torre Argentina 52 ☎ 06 6880 4601 🚋 To Largo di Torre Argentina

Colosseo

One of the best venues for seeing works by young Italian directors and playwrights.

✉ Via Capo d'Africa 5a ☎ 06 700 4932 Ⓜ Colosseo 🚋 81, 85

Eliseo

One of Rome's main venues, founded as an open-air theatre at the beginning of the 20th century. The theatre features some of the best Italian talent in various plays by Italian playwrights and adaptations of foreign works.

✉ Via Nazionale 183 ☎ 06 4887 2222 Ⓜ Repubblica 🚋 To Via Nazionale

Olimpico

A vast barn of a place where international dance and musical productions are staged. It is also where the Rome Philharmonic Orchestra holds its concerts.
✉ Piazza Gentile da Fabriano 17 ☎ 06 326 5991 🚌 To Piazza Mancini

Sistina

This is the place to come, just off Piazza Spagna, for musicals, either homegrown or Italianized versions of London and New York hits.
✉ Via Sistina 129 ☎ 06 420711 Ⓜ Barberini 🚌 To Piazza Barberini

Valle

One of two venues for the National Italian Theatre company. Excellent productions of modern classics such as Pirandello, Beckett and Pinter and occasional English plays by visiting companies.
✉ Via del Teatro Valle 23a ☎ 06 6880 3794 🚌 To Corso Vittorio Emanuele

Vascello

As well as hosting some of the most interesting theatre companies in Italy, this is a venue for ballet, contemporary and ethnic dance.
✉ Via Giacinto Carini 72 ☎ 06 588 1021 🚌 41, 44, 75

Music: Classical and Opera

Auditorio di Santa Cecilia

The Accademia has one of Rome's best chamber and symphony orchestras, who perform here, often under the baton of top-class visiting conductors.
✉ Via della Conciliazione 4 ☎ 06 6880 1044 🚌 To Piazza del Risorgimento

Parco della Musica

Rome's premier auditorium for classical concerts.

Designed by Renzo Piano this venue has three performances areas, which includes an outdoor arena. It is expected bodies such as the Accademia Nazionale di Santa Cecilia will perform here.
✉ Viale Pietro de Coubertin 15 ☎ 06 8024 1281 🚌 To Viale Pietro de Coubertin

Teatro Olimpico

Where the Filarmonica di Roma, and its visiting performers and ensembles, perform. (➤ Theatre and Dance, above).

Teatro dell'Opera

The winter season of the Rome opera and ballet company takes place here. In summer (mid-Jun and Aug) performances are staged in the Piazza di Siena, in the Villa Borghese.
✉ Via Firenze 72 ☎ 06 4816 0255/481 7003; www.opera.roma.it Ⓜ Termini 🚌 To Termini,

Music: Jazz, Rock

Alexanderplatz

The place for jazz in Rome. In its 16 years it has hosted top-quality acts. A restaurant and cocktail bar.
✉ Via Ostia 9 ☎ 06 3974 2171 Ⓜ Ottaviano 🚌 To Largo Trionfale

Alpheus

Three separate areas: one catering for jazz, one for rock and the other for dancing to records.
✉ Via del Commercio 36 ☎ 06 574 7826 Ⓜ Piramide 🚌 To Via Ostiense

Be Bop

Exclusively staging jazz and blues, this club, located in Testaccio, promotes both Italian and international acts in a comfortable venue.
✉ Via Giulietti 14 ☎ 06 5728 8959 Ⓜ Piramide 🚌 To Testaccio

Ancient Theatre

For an authentic ancient Roman theatre experience head down to the well-preserved ancient Roman theatre at Ostia Antica (➤ 86) in July and August when the Teatro Romano produces classical Roman and Greek plays. Alternatively, at the Vatican end of the Gianicolo (➤ 43) lies the little amphitheatre of Tasso's Oak, where ancient and less ancient classics are performed against the backdrop of wonderful views of the city.

Anfiteatro della Quercia del Tasso

✉ Passegiata del Gianicolo ☎ 06 575 0827 🕐 Jul–Sep 🚌 44, 75 Teatro Romano di Ostia Antica 🚌 Vilae dei Romagnoli 717, Ostia Antica ☎ 06 5635 8099 🕐 Jul–Aug 🚂 Train to Ostia Antica

Big Mama

Sub-titled 'the home of the blues in Rome', Big Mama has an interesting agenda of live music performed by Italian and international musicians, including the occasional legend.
✉ Vicolo San Francesco a Ripa 18 ☎ 06 581 2551 🚌 To Viale di Trastevere

Music, Clubs, Bars & Sport

Outdoor Music
During the summer there are plenty of outdoor classical musical events, including a series of Sunday morning concerts given by the orchestras of various branches of the armed forces on the Pincio. For a combination of world-class performers and a staggeringly beautiful setting, head to Villa Giulia (➤ 78) which is where the Accademia di Santa Cecilia hosts its summer season. Other top-quality performers can be heard under the remains of Teatro di Marcello (➤ 74).

Teatro di Marcello
✉ Via del Teatro di Marcello ☎ Information about the concerts: 06 481 4800 🚆 To Via del Teatro di Marcello

Terme di Caracalla
✉ Via della Terme di Caracalla 52 ☎ Box office: Teatro dell'Opera 06 481601 🕐 Jun–Oct 🚆 To Termi di Caracalla ♿ Few

Villa Giulia
✉ Piazzale di Villa Giulia 9 ☎ Information about the concerts: 06 678 6428 🕐 Jul 🚆 To Via Flaminia, Viale delle Belle Arti

Circolo degli Artisti
Some of the most recent big names from the international music scene play here. It is also a good place for dancing and organizes nights of 1960s, African and so on music, as well as hosting visiting DJs from the rest of Europe.
✉ Via Casilina Vecchia 42 ☎ 06 7030 5684

Gregory's
Drink Guinness while you indulge in some good live jazz. A pleasant venue near the Spanish Steps.
✉ Via Gregoriana 54d ☎ 06 679 6386 🚇 Barberini 🚆 To Piazza di Spagna

Jive
Get some of the latest sounds in Rome at this exciting venue close to Piazza Navona with an outdoor area for concerts in summer months.
✉ Via Guiseppe Libetta 7 ☎ 06 574 5989 🚇 Garbatella 🚆 To Via Ostiense

Il Locale
Small, friendly venue near Piazza Navona with mainly Italian live music.
✉ Vicolo del Fico 3 ☎ 06 687 9075 🚆 To Corso Vittorio Emanuele

Palalottomatica
Rome's largest music venue is in the 1960 Olympic Piazzale dello Sport. Big international names have appeared here such as the Rolling Stones, and top acts continue to come. Also festivals, eight restaurants and numerous bars.
✉ Piazzale dello Sport ☎ 199 128800 🚇 EUR Palasport

Stadio Olimpico
A sports stadium that hosts the very biggest Italian and foreign rock names to come to Rome.
✉ Via dei Gladiatori ☎ 06 323 7333 🚆 To Lungotevere Maresciallo Cadorna

Stazione Ouagadougou
Offers live and recorded African music in a spectacularly furnished venue. African snacks and beer too. Very friendly staff.
✉ Via della Lungaretta 75 ☎ 06 659 0030 🚆 To Viale di Trastevere

Nightclubs and Bars

Alibi
A hetero-friendly gay club in the throbbing Testaccio area.
✉ Via di Monte Testaccio 44 ☎ 06 574 3448 🚇 Piramide 🚆 To Via Marmorata

Alien
Vast mainstream disco with *cubistes* (scantily clad girls, and a few boys, who dance on top of columns for those who cannot be bothered to move themselves).
✉ Via Velletri 13 ☎ 06 841 2212 🚆 To Piazza Fiume

Caffè Latino
One of the earliest of the Testaccio clubs to open. In spite of its name you're as likely to hear jazz, blues or rock music as you are Latin American.
✉ Via di Monte Testaccio 96 ☎ 06 5728 8556 🚇 Piramide 🚆 To Via Marmorata

Escopazzo
A popular '30-somethings' wine and cocktail bar in the

heart of the city. Live music from Wednesday to Saturday night. Nice ambience and good food, too.

✉ Via d'Aracoeli 41 ☎ 06 6920 0422 🚌 To Piazza Venezia

Gilda

The establishment place to bop (or watch others), frequented by, among others, right-wing politicians and TV personalities.

✉ Via Mario de' Fiori 97 ☎ 06 678 4838 🚌 To Piazza San Silvestro

Goa

One of Rome's trendiest and most stylish nightclubs. Inspired by Southeast Asia, this is a cool place to hang out and attracts some of Europe's top DJs. House, hip-hop, jungle and tribal music predominate.

✉ Via Libetta 13 ☎ 06 574 8277 🚌 To Via Ostiense

Jonathan's Angels

A beautifully decorated cocktail bar, covered with the paintings of its biker owner, Jonathan.

✉ Via della Fossa 16 ☎ 06 689 3426 🚌 To Corso del Rinascimento, Corso Vittorio Emanuele

Piper

The place of the Dolce Vita 1960s; now a non-threatening club for those who do not do much clubbing.

✉ Via Tagliamento 9 ☎ 06 841 4459 🚌 To Via Tagliamento

Sport

Cavalieri Hilton

At a price you can enjoy the luxury of the Hilton's outdoor swimming pool.

✉ Via Cadlolo 101 ☎ 06 3509 2950 🕐 May–Sept: 9–7 🚌 To Piazzale Medaglie d'Oro

Circolo del Golf di Roma

A beautiful 18-hole course surrounded by pine trees and Roman ruins. Good on-site restaurant.

✉ Via Appia Nuova 716a ☎ 06 780 3407 🕐 Tue–Sun 8–sunset 🚇 Colli Albani, then taxi ride

Foro Italico

The annual International Tennis Tournament, the Italian Open, is held here for two weeks in mid-May.

✉ Viale dei Gladiatori 31 ☎ 06 36851/3685 8218 🚌 To Lungotevere Maresciallo Cadorna

Il Galoppatoio

For equestrian lovers; horse-riding classes to suit all levels.

✉ Via del Galoppatoio 25 ☎ 06 322 6797 🚌 To Via Veneto

Ippodromo delle Campanelle

This is Rome's horse-racing track. Races are held from September to June.

✉ Via Appia Nuova 1255 ☎ 06 718 8750 🚌 To Via Appia Nuova

Piscina delle Rose

Aptly named public swimming pool where you can rent sun-beds and umbrellas. There is also a bar.

✉ Viale America 20 ☎ 06 592 6717 🚇 EUR Palasport 🚌 To Piazzale dello Sport

Roman Sport Centre

Daily membership allows you access to the gyms of one of Rome's most exclusive sports and fitness clubs.

✉ The car park underneath Villa Borghese ☎ 06 320 1667/321 8096 🕐 Mon–Sat 9am–10pm, Sun 9–3 🚇 Spagna 🚌 To Via Veneto

Stadio Olimpico

Both the football teams, AS Roma and Lazio play here.

✉ Via dei Gladiatori ☎ 06 3685 7520 🚌 To Lungotevere Maresciallo Cadorna

Swim, Sun, Sand

It may not be the best way to escape the crowds, but a day at the beach is a good break from sightseeing, especially during the week. Entrepreneurs sometimes limit beach access to those renting sunbeds and parasols, but this is not always the case. Bars and restaurants offer lunch. The nearest beaches are at Ostia (metro from Magliana), Fregene and Torvaianica. Further afield are Sperlonga (➤ 87) to the south and Santa Marinella to the north.

What's On When

Villaggio Globale
The old abattoir in the centre of Testaccio has been taken over and converted into the Villaggio Globale, a cultural venue for exhibitions, concerts and dance events. In the summer the vast central courtyard (originally used for herding animals) is given over to an excellent festival of world music with side stalls and an interesting range of international refreshment stands.

✉ Lungotevere Testaccio
☎ 06 575 7233 🚌 27, 92 to Lungotevere Testaccio

January
New Year's Day: public holiday.
6 Jan: Epiphany, public holiday. Traditionally the *befana* (witch) leaves presents for children.

February
Week leading up to Shrove Tuesday: *Carnevale* (➤ 111), streets full of adults and children in fancy dress.
Shrove Tuesday: *Martedi grasso* celebrations (in costume) in Piazza Navona (➤ 21) and elsewhere.

March/April
9 Mar: cars, buses and taxis blessed at the church of San Francesca Romana (the patron saint of motorists) in the Forum (➤ 22).
Mid-Mar onwards: Spanish Steps (➤ 60) decorated with huge azalea plants.
Good Friday: Pope leads the ceremony of the Stations of the Cross at the Colosseo (Colosseum) (➤ 18).
Easter Sunday: papal address at St. Peter's.
Easter Monday: public holiday.
21 Apr: Rome's birthday, bands and orchestras perform at Campidoglio, (➤ 16) Piazza di Spagna (➤ 60) and elsewhere.
25 Apr: Liberation Day, public holiday to commemorate the Allies' liberation of Rome from the Nazis in 1944.

May
1 May: Labour Day, public holiday, no public transportation, huge free rock concert in Piazza di San Giovanni in Laterano.
Early May: horse show at Piazza di Siena.

Mid-May to Oct: rose garden above Circo Massimo (➤ 39) open to the public.
Mid-May: International Tennis Tournament (➤ 115).

June/July
Mid-Jun to Sep: outdoor concerts, cinemas, fairs and other arts events all over the city.
End-Jun to mid-Sep: *Estate Romana*. The ever expanding festival offering open-air cinema, music, theatre and arts events around the city.
Mid to late Jul: *Festa de Noantri*, stalls, concerts and other cultural events in Trastevere.

August
15 Aug: *Ferragosto*, public holiday, lots of shops, restaurants, bars and businesses close for a week or more.

October
Early Oct: wine festivals in towns near Rome, and a small one in Trastevere.

November
1 Nov: All Saints, public holiday.
Mid-Nov: the new season's *vini novelli* ready for drinking.

December
Beginning Dec to 6 Jan: Christmas fair in Piazza Navona (➤ 21, 110).
8 Dec: Immaculate Conception, public holiday.
Christmas time: *presepi* (nativity scenes) on show in churches and main piazzas.
25 Dec: Christmas Day, public holiday, papal address in St. Peter's Square.
31 Dec: New Year's Eve celebrations, fireworks and concerts in Piazza del Popolo and elsewhere in the city.

Practical Matters

Before You Go 118
When You Are There 119–123
Language 124

Above: *Fusilli pasta*
Below: *Roman police*

TIME DIFFERENCES

GMT	Rome	Germany	USA (NY)	Netherlands	Spain
12 noon	1pm	1pm	7am	1pm	1PM

BEFORE YOU GO

WHAT YOU NEED

	UK	Germany	USA	Netherlands	Spain
● Required ○ Suggested ▲ Not required — Some countries require a passport to remain valid for a minimum period (usually at least six months) beyond the date of entry—contact their consulate or embassy or your travel agent for details.					
Passport or National Identity Card where applicable	●	●	●	●	●
Visa (Regulations can change, please check before your journey)	▲	▲	▲	▲	▲
Onward or Return Ticket	▲	▲	▲	▲	▲
Health Inoculations	▲	▲	▲	▲	▲
Health Documentation (reciprocal agreement document) (▶ 123, Health)	●	●	▲	●	●
Travel Insurance	○	○	○	○	○
Driving Licence (national)	●	●	●	●	●
Car Insurance Certificate (if own car)	○	○	○	○	○
Car Registration Document (if own car)	●	●	●	●	●

WHEN TO GO

Rome

■ High season
▢ Low season

7°C	8°C	11°C	14°C	18°C	23°C	26°C	25°C	22°C	18°C	13°C	9°C
JAN	FEB	MAR	APR	MAY	JUN	JUL	AUG	SEP	OCT	NOV	DEC

☁ Wet ☁ Cloud ☀ Sun

TOURIST OFFICES

In the UK
Italian State Tourist Board
1 Princes Street
London W1R 2AY
☎ 020 7408 1254
Fax: 020 7399 3567

In the USA
Italian State Tourist Board
630 Fifth Avenue
Suite 1565
New York NY 10111
☎ 212/245 4822
Fax: 212/586 9249

Italian State Tourist Board
12400 Wilshire Boulevard
Suite 550
Los Angeles, CA 90025
☎ 310/820 0098
Fax: 310/820 6357

POLICE 113 CARABINIERI 112

FIRE 115

ANY EMERGENCY (including AMBULANCE) 118

ROAD ASSISTANCE (ACI) 116

WHEN YOU ARE THERE

ARRIVING

There are direct flights from Europe and North America. Alitalia (☎ 06 65641) is the national airline. Rome has two airports: Leonardo da Vinci, also known as Fiumicino (☎ 06 65951), is the larger and handles scheduled flights, while Ciampino (☎ 06 794941) caters mostly for charter flights.

Leonardo da Vinci (Fiumicino) Airport
Kilometres to city centre   Journey times

36 kilometres (22 miles)

🚆	30 or 45 minutes
🚌	50 minutes
🚗	40 minutes

Ciampino Airport
Kilometres to city centre   Journey times

15 kilometres (9 miles)

🚆	20 minutes after bus
🚌	15 minutes (to train)
🚗	30 minutes

MONEY

The euro (€) is the official currency of Italy. Euro banknotes and coins were introduced in January 2002. Banknotes are issued in denominations of 5, 10, 20, 50, 100, 200 and 500 euros; coins in denominations of 1, 2, 5, 10, 20 and 50 cents; and 1 and 2 euros.

TIME

 Italy is one hour ahead of Greenwich Mean Time (GMT+1), but from late March, when clocks are put forward one hour, to late September, Italian Summer Time (GMT+2) operates.

CUSTOMS

 **YES
From another EU country for** personal use (guidelines):
800 cigarettes, 200 cigars, 1 kilogram of tobacco
10 litres of spirits (over 22%)
20 litres of aperitifs
90 litres of wine, of which 60 litres can be sparkling wine
110 litres of beer

From a non-EU country for your personal use, the allowances are:
200 cigarettes OR
50 cigars OR 20 grams of tobacco
1 litre of spirits (over 22%)
2 litres of intermediary products (e.g. sherry) and sparkling wine
2 litres of still wine
50 grams of perfume
0.25 litres of eau de toilette
The value limit for goods is 175 euros

Travellers under 17 years of age are not entitled to the tobacco and alcohol allowances

 NO
Drugs, firearms, ammunition, offensive weapons, obscene material, unlicensed animals.

EMBASSIES

UK	**Germany**	**USA**	**Netherlands**	**Spain**
4220 0001	492131	46741	322 141	684 0401

WHEN YOU ARE THERE

TOURIST OFFICES

Ente Provinciale Tourismo (Rome Provincial Tourist Board)

Visitor Centres:
- Via Parigi 11
  ☎ 06 3660 4399/06 488991
  ◑ Mon–Sat 9–7

- Leonardo da Vinci (Fiumicino) Airport
  ☎ 06 3600 4399
  ◑ Mon–Sun 8–7

- Stazione Termini (Main Railway Station)
  ☎ 06 4890 6300
  ◑ 8am–9pm

Info-Tourism Kiosks:
◑ 9–6

- Largo Carlo Goldoni, Via del Corso
  ☎ 06 6813 6061

- Palazzo delle Esposizioni, Via Nazionale
  ☎ 06 4782 4525

- Fori Imperiali
  Piazza del Tempio della Pace ☎ 06 6992 4307

- Fontana di Trevi
  Via Marco Minghetti
  ☎ 06 678 2988

- Santa Maria Maggiore
  Via dell'Olmata
  ☎ 06 474 0995

- Trastevere
  Piazza Sonnio
  ☎ 06 5833 3457

NATIONAL HOLIDAYS

J	F	M	A	M	J	J	A	S	O	N	D
2		1	2	1			1			1	3

1 Jan	New Year's Day
6 Jan	Epiphany
Mar/Apr	Easter Monday
25 Apr	Liberation Day, 1945
1 May	Labour Day
15 Aug	Assumption of the Virgin
1 Nov	All Saints' Day
8 Dec	Immaculate Conception
25 Dec	Christmas Day
26 Dec	St. Stephen's Day

Banks, businesses and most shops and museums close on these days. Rome celebrates its patron saint (St. Peter) on 29 June, but generally most places remain open.

OPENING HOURS

○ Shops ● Museums
● Offices ◑ Archeological Sites
● Banks ○ Churches

| 8am | 9am | 10am | NOON | 2pm | 4pm | 6pm | 8pm | 10pm |

☐ Day ☐ Mid day

In addition to the times in the chart, department stores, some supermarkets, plus shops in tourist areas may not close lunchtime, and sometimes remain open until later in the evening. Some shops shut Monday morning and in summer may close Saturday afternoon. Most shops close Sunday. Some banks open until 2pm and do not reopen in the afternoon. All are closed weekends.
Some museums also open in the afternoon (usually 5–8pm). Many museums close early on Sunday (around 1pm) and most are closed Mondays.

DRIVE ON THE RIGHT

Lavatories CHARGE

PUBLIC TRANSPORTATION

Internal Flights Services throughout the country are provided by Alitalia—he national airline (☎ 06 65641). The flight time to Rome from Milan is 65 minutes; from Florence 75 minutes; and from Naples 45 minutes. Departures are *Partenze Nazionali*, arrivals *Arrivi Nazionali*.

Trains Italian State Railways (Ferrovie dello Stato, or FS) provide an efficient service. Almost all long-distance trains to Rome arrive and depart from Stazione Termini (some fast trains use Stazione Roma Tiburtina). Stazione Termini is shut from midnight to 5am, then trains stop at other city stations. Timetable information ☎ 848 888088

Long Distance Buses There is no national bus company but COTRAL (☎ 800 150008, Mon–Sat) has the major presence in Rome, serving the Lazio region. Buses depart from numerous points throughout the city, depending on their destinations. For details ask at the nearest tourist information office.

Urban Transport Buses (yellow), plus in the outer districts trams, are the best way to get around, though the complexity of the routes can be daunting. Bus or tram stops (*fermata*) have yellow signs. You must have a ticket before boarding at the rear (*salita*) and your ticket stamped in the machine there. Exit through the middle door (*uscita*). The underground (*Metropolitana* or *Metrò*)—entrances: white 'M' on red—has only two lines: *Linea A* (red) runs from Battistini to Anagnina in the southeast. *Linea B* (blue) runs from Rebibbia in the northeast to Laurentina in the southwest. Tickets from machines at stations.

CAR RENTAL

Car hire (*autonoleggio*) is at airports, the main rail station, and city offices, but driving in Rome is not recommended and not cheap. Small local firms offer the best rates but cars can only be booked locally. Air or train travellers can benefit from inclusive deals.

TAXIS

Taxis can be hailed on the street, found at a taxi rank (stations and major piazze), or phoned 06 3570, 88177, 4994 or 5551). There is an initial charge and a rate for each kilometre. Traffic can mean stiff meter increases and there are Sunday and late-night supplements.

DRIVING

Speed limits on motorways (*autostrade*), which have tolls: **130kph/ 80mph**

Speed limits on main roads: **110kph/68mph**; secondary roads: **90kph/55mph**

Speed limits on urban roads: **50kph/30mph**

Must be worn in front seats at all times and in rear seats where fitted.

Random breath-testing. Never drive under the influence of alcohol.

Fuel (*benzina*) is more expensive in Italy than in Britain and most other European countries. All except small garages in out-of-the-way places sell unleaded fuel (*senza piombo*). Outside urban areas filling stations open 7am to 12.30pm and 3 to 7.30pm. Motorway service stations are open 24 hours. Credit cards arenot widely accepted.

In the event of a breakdown, ring 116, giving your registration number and type of car and the nearest ACI (Automobile Club d'Italia) office will be informed to assist you. You will be towed to the nearest ACI garage. This service is free to foreign-registered vehicles or cars rented from Rome or Milan airports (you will need to produce your passport).

PERSONAL SAFETY

In Rome, petty theft (bag and neck-chain snatching, pick-pocketing and car break-ins) is the main problem. The police (*polizia*) to whom thefts should be reported wear light-blue trousers and dark-blue jackets. Some precautions:
- Carry shoulder bags not *on* your shoulder but slung *across* your body.
- Scooter-borne bag-snatchers can be foiled if you keep on the *inside* of the pavement.
- Do not put anything down on a café or restaurant table.
- Lock car doors and never keep valuables in your car.

Police assistance:
☎ **113** from any call box

TELEPHONES

Almost every bar in Italy has a telephone, plus many in public places. Phonecards are available from SIP (state telephone company) offices, tobacconists, stations and other public places. Coin operated telephones are now rare.

International Dialling Codes	
From Rome to:	
UK:	**00 44**
Germany:	**00 49**
USA:	**00 1**
Netherlands:	**00 31**
Spain:	**00 34**

POST

Post Offices
The city's main post office is on Piazza San Silvestro 19.
🕐 8.30–7.30 (8.30–1 Sat).
Closed: Sun
☎ 800 160000
Vatican City has its own postal system, with a post office in St. Peter's Square.
🕐 8.30–7 (6 Sat)
Closed: Sun ☎ 06 9888 3406

ELECTRICITY

The power supply is: 220 volts (in parts of Rome: 125 volts).

Type of socket: Round two- or three-hole sockets takings plugs of two round pins, or sometimes three pins in a vertical row. British visitors should bring an adaptor; US visitors a voltage transformer.

TIPS/GRATUITIES

Yes ✓ No ✗		
Hotels (if service not included)	✓	10–15%
Restaurants (if service not included)	✓	10–15%
Cafés/bars	✓	€1 min
Taxis	✓	15%
Porters	✓	€1
Chambermaids	✓	€0.50–€1
Cinema/theatre usherettes	✓	10 cents min
Hairdressers	✓	€2
Cloakroom attendants	✓	€1
Lavatories	✓	10 cents min

PHOTOGRAPHY

Light: The light in Rome is good: neither the glare of the south nor the hazier light of the north of the country.

Where you can photograph: Most museums and certain churches will not allow you to photograph inside; check first.

Film and developing: A roll of film is called a *pellicola*, but 'film' should get you understood. Film and developing are much more expensive in Italy than in the UK or USA.

HEALTH

Insurance
Nationals of EU and certain other countries receive reduced cost medical (including hospital) treatment and pay a percentage of prescribed medicines. You need a qualifying document (Form E111 for Britons). Private medical insurance is still advised.

Dental Services
Nationals of EU and certain other countries can obtain dental treatment at a reduced cost at dentists within the Italian health service. A qualifying document (Form E111 for Britons) is needed. Private medical insurance is still advised.

Sun Advice
In summer, particularly in July and August, it can get oppressively hot and humid in the city. If 'doing the sights' cover up or apply a sunscreen (or dive into the shade of a museum), plus take in plenty of fluids.

Drugs
A pharmacy (*farmacia*), recognized by a green cross sign, will possess highly trained staff able to offer medical advice on minor ailments and provide a wide range of prescribed and non-prescribed medicines and drugs.

Safe Water
Rome is famed for its drinking water, which is generally safe, even from outdoor fountains (unless you see a sign saying *acqua non potabile*). However, Romans prefer the taste of bottled mineral

CONCESSIONS

Students/Youths Holders of an International Student Identity Card (ISIC), and for those under 26 an International Youth Card (IYC)—vailable from student organizations—can take advantage of discounts on transportation, accommodation, museum entrance fees, car rental and in restaurants. Nationals (under 18) of EU and certain other countries receive free admission to state museums.

Senior Citizens Citizens aged over 60 of EU and a number of other countries with which Italy has a reciprocal arrangement (not including the USA) may gain free admission to communal and state museums and receive discounts at other museums and on public transport on production of their passport.

CLOTHING SIZES

Italy	UK	Rest of Europe		
46	36	46	36	Suits
48	38	48	38	
50	40	50	40	
52	42	52	42	
54	44	54	44	
56	46	56	46	
41	7	41	8	Shoes
42	7.5	42	8.5	
43	8.5	43	9.5	
44	9.5	44	10.5	
45	10.5	45	11.5	
46	11	46	12	
37	14.5	37	14.5	Shirts
38	15	38	15	
39/40	15.5	39/40	15.5	
41	16	41	16	
42	16.5	42	16.5	
43	17	43	17	
38	8	34	6	Dresses
40	10	36	8	
42	12	38	10	
44	14	40	12	
46	16	42	14	
48	18	44	16	
38	4.5	38	6	Shoes
38	5	38	6.5	
39	5.5	39	7	
39	6	39	7.5	
40	6.5	40	8	
41	7	41	8.5	

WHEN DEPARTING

- Contact the airport or airline on the day prior to leaving to ensure the flight details are unchanged.
- The airport departure tax, payable when you leave Italy, is included in the cost of the airline ticket.
- Check the duty-free limits of the country you are travelling to before departure.

LANGUAGE

Italian is the native language but Romans speak a dialect with its own particular stresses, intonations and vocabulary, of which they are fiercely proud. Many Romans speak English but you will be better received if you at least attempt to communicate in Italian. Italian words are pronounced phonetically. Every vowel and consonant (except 'h') is sounded. The accent usually (but not always) falls on the penultimate syllable. Below is a list of a few words that may be helpful. More extensive coverage can be found in the AA's *Essential Italian Phrase Book* which lists over 2,000 phrases and 2,000 words.

hotel	*albergo*	breakfast	*prima colazione*
room	*camera*	toilet	*toilette*
..single/double	*....singola/doppia*	bath	*bagno*
..one/two nights	*per una/due notte/i*	shower	*doccia*
		balcony	*balcone*
..one/two people	*....per una/due persona/e*	reception	*reception*
		key	*chiave*
reservation	*prenotazione*	room service	*servizio da camera*
rate	*tariffa*	chambermaid	*cameriera*

bank	*banco*	bank note	*banconota*
exchange office	*cambio*	coin	*moneta*
post office	*posta*	credit card	*carta di credito*
cashier	*cassiere/a*	traveller's cheque	*assegno turistico*
foreign exchange	*cambio con l'estero*	cheque book	*libretto degli assegni*
foreign currency	*valuta estera*		
pound sterling	*sterlina*	exchange rate	*tasso di cambio*
American dollar	*dollaro*	commission charge	*commissione*

restaurant	*ristorante*	starter	*il primo*
café	*caffè*	main course	*il secondo*
table	*tavolo*	dish of the day	*piatto del giorno*
menu	*menù/carta*	dessert	*dolci*
set menu	*menù turístico*	drink	*bevanda*
wine list	*lista dei vini*	waiter	*cameriere*
lunch	*pranzo/colazione*	waitress	*cameriera*
dinner	*cena*	the bill	*conto*

aeroplane	*aeroplano*	..single/return	*....andata sola/ andata e ritorno*
airport	*aeroporto*		
train	*treno*	...first/second class	*....prima/seconda classe*
..station	*....stazione ferroviaria*		
		ticket office	*biglietteria*
bus	*autobus*	timetable	*orario*
..station	*....autostazione*	seat	*posto*
ferry	*traghetto*	non-smoking	*vietato fumaro*
ticket	*biglietto*	reserved	*prenotato*

yes	*sì*	help!	*aiuto!*
no	*no*	today	*oggi*
please	*per favore*	tomorrow	*domani*
thank you	*grazie*	yesterday	*ieri*
hello	*ciao*	how much?	*quanto?*
goodbye	*arrivederci*	expensive	*caro*
goodnight	*buona notte*	open	*aperto*
sorry	*mi dispiace*	closed	*chiuso*

INDEX

INDEX

Accademia di San Luca 32
accommodation 100–103
Albano Laziale 85
Antiquario Comunale 32
Appian Way 62, 110
Aquafelix 111
Aquapiper 111
Appartamento Borgia 32
Arch of Septimius Severus 22
Arch of Titus 22
Arco di Costantino 33
Ariccia 81, 85

Banditaccia Necropolis 82
banks 120
bars 7, 114–115
Basilica Aemilia 22
Basilica Julia 22
Basilica of Maxentius and
   Constantine 22
Basilica di San Giovanni e
   Paolo 33
Basilica di Santa Maria
   Maggiore 36
Basilica di San Paolo fuori le
   Mura 36
Basilica di San Sebastiano
   36–37
beaches 115
Bernini, Gian Lorenzo 21, 26,
   42, 57, 61, 63, 65, 70, 71,
   72
Bocca della Verità 68
Bomarzo 81
buses 121

Campidoglio 16
Campo de'Fiori 37
Capitoline Museums 16
Caprarola 82
Caravaggio 14, 42, 63, 68, 70
Carcere Mamertino 46
Carnevale 111
Castel Gandolfo 85
Castel Sant'Angelo 17, 110
Castelli Romani 85
catacombs of San Callisto 37
catacombs of Santa Priscilla 38
cats, street 12
Cecilia Metella, tomb of 62
Celian hill 67
Cerveteri 82
Chiesa Nuova 38
children's attractions 110–111
Christina of Sweden, Queen
   14, 53
churches 7, 35
   see also individual entries
cinema 112
Circo Massimo 12, 39
Civitavecchia 83
climate 7, 118, 123
clothing sizes 123
Colle Oppio 12
Colosseum (Colosseo) 12, 18,
   110

Column of Marcus Aurelius 39
Constantine's Arch 33
crime 7
Curia 22
customs regulations 119

departure information 124
Domine Quo Vadis 62
Domus Aurea 39
drives
   Castelli Romani 85
   Etruria 83

eating out 34, 50–51, 92–99
embassies 120
emergency numbers 119, 122
entertainment 112–116
Etruria 83

famous residents and visitors
   14
festivals and events 116
Fontana delle Api 57
Fontana della Barcaccia 61
Fontana dei Fiumi 21
Fontana delle Naiadi 59
Fontana Paola 44
Fontana delle Tartarughe 39
Fontana di Trevi 9, 40
food and drink 50–51, 92–99
Fori Imperiali 13, 40
Foro Romano 22
Fosse Ardeatine 62
Frascati 84

Galleria Borghese 42
Galleria Nazionale d'Arte
   Moderna e Contemporanea
   42
Galleria Spada 56, 110
Il Gesù 43
Ghetto 43, 44
Gianicolo 43, 44
Giardino Zoologico 111
Grottaferrata 85

health 118, 123
history 10–11

ice-cream 35
Isola Tiberina 44, 45

Keats-Shelley Memorial House
   45

language 124
Largo Argentina 45, 110
lavatories 121
leisure activities 34–35
local ways and etiquette 34
Luna Park 111

Mamertine Prison 46
maps
   central Rome 28–29
   excursions 81
   shopping 76–77
   Vatican 73

Marino 85
markets 109
Mercati Traiano 46
Michelangelo 14, 16, 24–25,
   26, 69, 71
money 119
Monumento a Vittorio
   Emanuele II 46
Museo dell'Alto Medioevo
   46–47
Museo delle Arti e Tradizioni
   Popolari 47
Museo Barracco 48
Museo delle Cere 110
Museo Chiaramonti 24
Museo della Civiltà Romana
   48, 110
Museuo di Roma in Trastevere
   48, 110–111
Museo Gregoriano-Egizio 24
Museo Gregoriano-Etrusco 24
Museo Nazionale delle Paste
   Alimentari 49
Museo Nazionale di Cerveteri
   82
Museo Nazionale di Tarquinia
   83
Museo Nazionale Romano 49
Museo Pio Clementine 24
Museo Civico di Zoologia 48
music venues 113, 114–115

Napoleon Bonaparte 14, 48
national holidays 121
Nemi 85
nightclubs 114–115

opera 113
opening hours 120
Orti Farnesiana 52
Ostia Antica 86–87, 110

Palatino 12, 52
Palazzo Altemps 59
Palazzo Barberini 19
Palazzo della Cancelleria 58
Palazzo Chigi 81
Palazzo Colonna 52
Palazzo dei Conservatori 16
Palazzo Corsini 53
Palazzo Doria Pamphilj 54
Palazzo delle Esposizioni 54
Palazzo Farnese 59
Palazzo Madama 54
Palazzo di Montecitorio 54–55
Palazzo Nuovo 16
Palazzo Pio Righetti 37
Palazzo del Quirinale 55
Palazzo Senatorio 16
Palazzo Spada 56
Palazzo Venezia 56
Pantheon 20
Parco Nazionale d'Abruzzo 13
Parco di San Alessio 12
parks and gardens 12
Pasquino 57
passports and visas 122
personal safety 122

Piazza Barberini 57
Piazza del Cavalieri di Malta 57
Piazza Farnese 12, 59
Piazza Giuseppe Garibaldi 43
Piazza Navona 21, 111
Piazza del Popolo 59
Piazza della Repubblica 59
Piazza di Spagna 60–61
Piazza Venezia 46
Pincio Gardens 59
Piramide Cestia 61
pizzas 97
police 122
Ponte Rotto 45
Ponte Sant'Angelo 61
the Pope 34, 85
population 7
Porta San Sebastiano 63
postal services 120, 122
Protestant Cemetery 63
public transport 121
puppet shows 111

Raphael 14, 19, 20, 24, 78
Rocca di Papa 85
Rocca Pia 88
Roman Forum 22

St. Peter 14, 46, 62
St. Peter's 9, 26
Sant'Agostino 63
Sant'Andrea al Quirinale 63
Sant'Andrea della Valle 64
San Bartolomeo 45
Santi Bonifacio e Alessio 67
San Carlo alle Quattro Fontane 64
Santa Cecilia in Trastevere 64
San Clemente 23, 110
San Crisogono 44
Santa Croce in Gerusalemme 65
San Francesco a Ripa 65

San Giovanni in Laterano 65
San Gregorio Magno 66
Sant'Ignazio di Loyola 66, 110
Sant'Ivo Alla Sapienz 66
San Luigi dei Francesi 68
Santa Maria della Concezione 68, 110
Santa Maria in Cosmedin 9, 68, 110
Santa Maria in Domnica 69
Santa Maria sopra Minerva 69
Santa Maria del Popolo 70
Santa Maria della Scala 44
Santa Maria in Trastevere 70–71
Santa Maria della Vittoria 71
San Pietro 9, 26
San Pietro in Montorio 71
San Pietro in Vincoli 71
Santa Prassede 72
Santa Pudenziana 72
Santi Quattro Coronati 73
Santa Sabina 73
Santo Stefano Rotondo 74
San Tommaso in Formis 67
shopping 104–109
Sistine Chapel 24–25
Spanish Steps 60
Sperlonga 87
sport 115

Tarquinia 83
taxis 121
Teatro di Marcello 74
telephones 122
Tempi di Vesta e della Fortuna Virilis 75
Temple of Castor and Pollux 22
Temple of Romulus 22
Temple of Vesta 22
Terme de Caracalla 12, 75
Testaccio 76–77
theatre and dance 112–113

time 118, 119
tipping 122
Tivoli 88
tourist offices 118, 120
trains 121
Trastevere 12
travelling to Rome 119
Trevi Fountain 9, 40
Tritone 57
Tuscania 83
Tusculum 84

VAT refunds 106
Vatican City 6
Vatican Museums 24
Via Appia Antica 62, 110
Via Condotti 77
Via Veneto 57
views of Rome 34
Villa Adriana 89
Villa Aldobrandini 84
Villa Borghese 12
Villa Celimontana 12
Villa Doria Pamphili 12
Villa d'Este 88
Villa Farnese 82
Villa Farnesina 78
Villa Giulia 78
Villa Gregoriana 88
Villa Sciarra 12
Villaggio Globale 116
Viterbo 90

walks
   from the Celian hill 67
   Gianicolo to the Ghetto 44
   historic centre 58
   Via Appia Antica 62
water parks 111
wildlife 12–13
wines and drinks 51, 84, 85

zoo 111

Acknowledgements
The Automobile Association wishes to thank the following libraries, photographers and associations for their assistance in the preparation of this book.

BRIDGEMAN ART LIBRARY/Vatican Museums and Galleries, Vatican City, Italy 24, 25, 27b; JOHN HESELTINE 90; MARY EVANS PICTURE LIBRARY 11,14; M R I BANKERS' GUIDE TO FOREIGN CURRENCY 119; SPECTRUM COLOUR LIBRARY 60, 89; THE STOCK MARKET, INC 27a; WORLD PICTURES LTD 12/3, 87.

The remaining transparencies are held in the Association's own library (**AA PHOTO LIBRARY**) with contributions from: **J Holmes t, B/cover 5a, 5b, 12, 16, 18, 26, 34, 35b, 39, 44, 47, 48, 49, 51a, 52, 55b, 57a, 57b, 59, 61, 65, 70, 72, 76; S McBride B/cover b; D Mitidieri F/cover (d) plaque, 7, 8a, 8b, 9a, 9b, 20, 23, 32, 35a, 36, 38, 42, 43, 56, 64, 66, 68, 69, 71, 74, 75a, 75b, 78a, 78b, 84a, 91a, 91b; C Sawyer B/cover ct, cb, 1,15b; 17, 21, 22, 31, 33, 41, 50a, 86, 117b; L B Smith 122a; T Souter 40, 53, 82, 83, 84b, 88, 117a; P Wilson F/cover 2, 6, 15a, 19, 37, 45, 50b, 55a, 62, 77, 79.**

Author's Acknowledgements
Jane Shaw wishes to thank Fiona Benson for expertise on churches, shops and hotels, Roberta Mitchell for expertise on restaurants and food and Sally Webb for expertise on museums and excursions.

The Automobile Association wishes to thank Marco De Pellegrin for his insight and invaluable assistance.

Contributors
Update and revision management: Apostrophe S Limited
Indexer: Marie Lorimer

Dear Essential Traveller

Your comments, opinions and recommendations are very important to us. So please help us to improve our travel guides by taking a few minutes to complete this simple questionnaire.

You do not need a stamp (unless posted outside the UK). If you do not want to cut this page from your guide, then photocopy it or write your answers on a plain sheet of paper.

Send to: **The Editor, AA World Travel Guides, FREEPOST SCE 4598, Basingstoke RG21 4GY.**

Your recommendations...

We always encourage readers' recommendations for restaurants, nightlife or shopping – if your recommendation is used in the next edition of the guide, we will send you a *FREE* AA *Essential* Guide of your choice. Please state below the establishment name, location and your reasons for recommending it.

_____

_____

_____

_____

Please send me **AA *Essential*** _____

About this guide...

Which title did you buy?
  AA *Essential* _____

Where did you buy it? _____

When? m m / y y

Why did you choose an AA *Essential* Guide? _____

_____

_____

_____

_____

Did this guide meet your expectations?
  Exceeded ☐   Met all ☐   Met most ☐   Fell below ☐
  Please give your reasons _____

_____

_____

_____

continued on next page...

Were there any aspects of this guide that you particularly liked? _____

_____

_____

Is there anything we could have done better? _____

_____

_____

About you…

Name (*Mr/Mrs/Ms*) _____

    Address _____

_____

_____ Postcode _____

    Daytime tel nos _____

Please only give us your mobile phone number if you wish to hear from us about other products and services from the AA and partners by text or mms.

Which age group are you in?
    Under 25 ☐ 25–34 ☐ 35–44 ☐ 45–54 ☐ 55–64 ☐ 65+ ☐

How many trips do you make a year?
    Less than one ☐ One ☐ Two ☐ Three or more ☐

Are you an AA member? Yes ☐ No ☐

About your trip…

When did you book? m m / y y   When did you travel? m m / y y

How long did you stay? _____

Was it for business or leisure? _____

Did you buy any other travel guides for your trip?

    If yes, which ones? _____

Thank you for taking the time to complete this questionnaire. Please send it to us as soon as possible, and remember, you do not need a stamp (*unless posted outside the UK*).

Happy Holidays!

ATLAS SYMBOLS

English / German		Italian / French
Motorway Autobahn		Autostrada Autoroute
Road with four lanes Vierspurige Straße		Strada a quattro corsie Route à quatre voies
Thoroughfare Durchgangsstraße		Strada di attraversamento Route de transit
Main road Hauptstraße		Strada principale Route principale
Other roads Sonstige Straßen		Altre strade Autres routes
Information Information		Informazioni Information
Parking place - Airport bus Parkplatz - Flughafenbus		Parcheggio - Autobus per l'aeroporto Parking - Bus d'aéroport
One-way street Einbahnstraße		Via a senso unico Rue à sens unique
Pedestrian zone Fußgängerzone		Zona pedonale Zone piétonne
Main railway with station Hauptbahn mit Bahnhof		Ferrovia principale con stazione Chemin de fer principal avec gare
Other railway Sonstige Bahn		Altra ferrovia Autre ligne
Underground U-Bahn		Metropolitana Métro
Tramway Straßenbahn		Tram Tramway
Church - Church of interest Kirche - Sehenswerte Kirche		Chiesa - Chiesa interessante Église -Église remarquable
Synagogue - Mosque Synagoge - Moschee		Sinagoga - Moschea Synagogue - Mosquée
Post office - Youth hostel Postamt - Jugendherberge		Ufficio postale - Ostello della gioventù Bureau de poste - Auberge de jeunesse
Police station - Hospital Polizei - Krankenhaus		Posto di polizia - Ospedale Poste de police - Hôpital
Monument - Well Denkmal - Brunnen		Monumento -Pozzo Monument - Puits
Tower Turm		Torre Tour
Built-up area, public building baute Fläche, öffentliches Gebäude		Caseggiato, edificio pubblico Zone bâtie, bâtiment public
Industrial area - Park, forest Industriegelände - Park, Wald		Zona industriale - Parco, bosco Zone industrielle - Parc, bois
Cemetery - Jewish cemetery Friedhof - Jüdischer Friedhof		Cimitero - Cimitero ebraico Cimetière - Cimetière juif
Restricted traffic zone one mit Verkehrsbeschränkungen		Zona con limitazioni di traffico Circulation réglementée par des péages

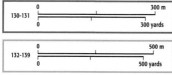

130-131 0 — 300 m / 0 — 300 yards

132-139 0 — 500 m / 0 — 500 yards

Rome Street Index

A

Acaia, Via **138**/D5-D6
Adda, Via **134**/C2
Adriana, Piazza **130**/A1-B2
Albalonga, Via **139**/E4-E5
Albania, Piazza **137**/F4
Albenga, Via **139**/F5
Alberico II, Via **132**/C4-C5
Alberto, Via Carlo **138**/C1
Aldrovandi, Via Ulisse **133**/F2-**134**/B1
Alessandria, Piazza **135**/E3
Alessandrina, Via **131**/F5
Alghero, Via **139**/F3
Altoviti, Lungotevere degli **130**/A2-A3
Amba Aradam, Via dell' **138**/C4-**139**/D3
Amendola, Via Giovanni **134**/C5-C6
Angelico, Borgo **132**/B4-C5
Angelico, Viale **132**/B1-B3
Anguillara, Lungotevere **137**/D2-E2
Anicia, Via **137**/D3
Anima, Via dell' **130**/C3-C4
Annibaldi, Via degli **138**/B1-B2
Anzani, Largo F. **137**/D4-D5
Aosta, Via **139**/E3-E4
Appia Antica, Via **139**/C6
Appia Nuova, Via **139**/E3-F5
Appia, Circonvallazione **139**/E6-F5
Appio, Piazzale **139**/D3-E3
Aprile,Viale XXI **135**/F1-F2
Aracoeli, Piazza d' **131**/E5
Aracoeli, Via dell' **131**/E5
Arancio, Via dell' **131**/D1
Archetto, Via dell' **131**/E3-F3
Arco d. Ciambel, Via dell' **131**/D4
Arco del Monte, Via **130**/C5
Arco di S. Calisto, Piazza d. **137**/D3
Arenula, Largo **131**/D5
Arenula, Via **130**/C6-**131**/D5
Armenia, Piazza **139**/E6
Armi, Lungotevere delle **133**/D2
Arnaldo da Brescia, Lungotevere **133**/D2-E3
Artigiani, Lungotevere degli **137**/D6
Artisti, Via d. **134**/A4
Asioli, Largo **134**/B1
Astalli, Via degli **131**/E4-E5
Augusta, Lungotevere **130**/C1-**133**/E4
Aurelia Antica, Via **136**/A2-B3
Aurelia, Via **132**/A6-B6
Aurelio, Piazzale **136**/B3
Aventina, Via **138**/A4-A5

Aventino, Lungotevere **137**/E3-F4
Aventino, Viale **137**/F4
Azuni, Via Domenico Alberto **133**/D2-E2

B

Babuino, Via del **133**/E3-F4
Baccarini, Via Alfredo **139**/F5-F6
Baccelli, Viale Guido **138**/A5-B6
Bainsizza, Piazza **132**/C1
Baldini, Via Baccio **136**/C6-**137**/D6
Balestrari **130**/C5
Banchi Nuovi, Via dei **130**/A3-A4
Barberini, Piazza **134**/A5
Barberini, Via **134**/A5-A6
Barbieri, Via **134**/B5-C5
Barchetta, Via della **130**/B4
Bari,Via **135**/E3
Barletta, Via **132**/B3
Barrili, Via Anton Giulio **136**/B4-B6
Bassi, Via Ugo **136**/C4
Battisti, Via Cesare **131**/E4-F4
Baullari, Via del **130**/B5-C4
Beccari, Viale Odoardo **138**/B6
Bellani, Via Angelo **136**/C6-**137**/D6
Belle Arti, Piazzale delle **133**/D1-D3
Belle Arti, Viale delle **133**/E1-F2
Belvedere, Via del **132**/B5
Benaglia, Via Francesco **136**/C5
Benedetta, Via **130**/B6
Bergamo, Via **134**/C3
Bernardino da Feltre, Piazza **136**/C4-**137**/D4
Bernini, Piazza Gian Lorenzo **138**/A5
Bianchi Vecchi, Via **130**/A3-B4
Biondo, Piazza Flavio **136**/C6
Bissolati, Via Leonida **134**/B4-B5
Bocca della Verità, Piazza **137**/E3
Bocca di Leone, Via **131**/E1-**133**/E4
Bodoni, Via Giovan Battista **137**/D5-E4
Boezio, Via **132**/C4-**133**/D4
Bolivar, Piazzale Simone **133**/F2
Bologna, Piazza **135**/F3
Bologna, Vicolo del **130**/B6
Boncompagni, Via **134**/B4-C4
Bonghi, Via Ruggero **138**/C2

Borghese, Piazz [...] **134**/B2
Borgognona, Via **131**/E1
Botteghe Oscure, Via delle **131**/D5-E5
Bottego, Piazza Vittorio **137**/E6
Branca, Via Giovanni **137**/D5-E4
Brasile, Piazza **134**/A3-A4
Brescia, Via **134**/C3
Bresciani, Via dei **130**/A4
Britannia, Via **139**/D5
Brofferio, Via Angelo **132**/C2-C3
Brunetti, Via Angelo **133**/E4
Buenos Aires, Piazza **134**/C2
Bufalo, Via del **131**/E2-F2
Buozzi, Viale Bruno **133**/E1-**134**/B1

C

Caio Cestio, Via **137**/E5
Cairoli, Piazza Benedetto **130**/C5
Calandrelli, Via **136**/B3-C3
Campania, Via **134**/A4-C3
Campidoglio, Piazza del **131**/E5-F5
Campitalli, Piazza di **131**/E5-E6
Campo Boario, Viale del **137**/E5-E6
Campo de' Fiori, Piazza **130**/C4-C5
Campo Marzio, Piazza **131**/D2
Campo Marzio, Via di **131**/D2
Cancelleria, Piazza della **130**/C4
Cancelleria, Via della **130**/B4
Candia, Via **132**/A4-B4
Capizucchi, Via **131**/E5
Capo le Case, Via **131**/F1-F2
Cappellari, Via dei **130**/B4
Capranica, Piazza **131**/D3
Carini, Via Giacinto **136**/B3-B4
Carlo Felice, Viale **139**/D3-E3
Caro, Via Lucrezio **133**/D4
Carovita, Via del **131**/E3
Carrozze, Via delle **131**/E1-F1
Carso, Viale **132**/B1-C1
Cartoni, Pietro, Via **136**/A6
Casilino, Via **139**/F2
Castaldi, Via Panfilo **136**/C6-**137**/D6
Castari, Via del **131**/D4
Castello, Lungotevere **130**/A2-B2
Castro Pretorio, Via **135**/D5
Castro Pretorio, Viale **135**/D4-D5
Catalana, Via **131**/D6
Catania, Via **135**/F3-F4

[...]canti, Via Guido **136**/B5-B6
Cavalieri di Vittorio Veneto, Viale dei **132**/A1-B2
Cavalieri, Via E. de **134**/B1
Cavalleggeri, Via di Porta **132**/A6-B6
Cavallini, Via Pietro **133**/E4
Cavallotti, Via Felice **136**/C5-C4
Cavour, Piazza **130**/B1
Cavour, Ponte **130**/C1
Cavour, Via **134**/C5-**138**/A1
Celimontana, Piazza **138**/B3
Celio Vibenna, Via **138**/B2
Cenci, Lungotevere dei **130**/C6-**131**/D6
Cenci, Piazza dei **130**/C6-**131**/D6
Cente Verde, Via **139**/D1-D3
Cerchi, Via dei **134**/C4-C5
Cernaia, Via **134**/C4-C5
Cerquetti, Via Damaso **136**/A6
Cerveteri, Via **139**/E4
Cesare, Viale Giulio **132**/B4-**133**/D3
Cesari, Via Antonio **136**/B4-B5
Cestari, Via de **131**/D4
Cestio, Ponte **137**/E2
Chiana, Via **135**/D1
Chiara, Via S. **131**/D4
Chiarini, Largo Giovanni **138**/B5
Chiavari, Largo d. **130**/C4
Chigi, Largo **131**/E2
Cicerone, Via **133**/D4
Cilicia, Via **138**/C6-**139**/D6
Cinque Giornate, Piazza delle **133**/D2-D3
Cinque Lune, Piazza delle **130**/C3
Cinque, Vicolo del **136**/C2-**137**/D2
Cinquecento, Piazza dei **134**/C5
Cipro, Via **134**/C5
Circo Massimo, Via del **132**/A4
Claudia, Via **138**/B2-B3
Clementino, Via del **131**/D2
Clodia, Circonvallazione **132**/A3-B1
Clodio, Piazzale **132**/B2
Cola di Rienzo, Piazza **132**/B4-**133**/D4
Colautti, Via Arturo **136**/B4
Coldoni, Largo **131**/D1
Collegio Romano, Piazza de **131**/E4
Collegio Romano, Via del **131**/E3-E4
Colo di Rienzo, Via **132**/B4-D4
Colombo, Via Cristoforo **138**/B6-C6
Colonna, Piazza **131**/E2-E3[...]

Colonna, Via Marcantonio 133/D3-D4

Colonna, Via Vittoria 130/B1-C1

Colosseo, Piazza del 138/B2

Conciliazione, Via della 132/B5-C5

Condotti, Via 131/E1

Confienza, Piazza 135/D5-E5

Conservatorio, Via del 130/C5-C6

Consolazione, Via della 131/E6-F6

Consulta, Via della 134/A6

Conte Verde, Via 139/D1-D2

Convertite, Via delle 131/E2

Coppelle, Via delle 130/C3-131/D3

Corallo, Via del 130/B3

Corda, Via d. 130/C5

Cornaro, Via Francesco 136/A5-B5

Coronari, Piazza 130/C5

Coronari, Via dei 130/A3-C3

Corr. Ricci, Largo 138/A1

Corridori, Via 132/B1-C1

Corsini, Via 130/A6

Corso d'Italia 135/D2

Corso, Via del 131/E4-133/E3

Costamagna, Piazza 131/D5

Cottolengo, Via del 132/A6

Crescenzi, Salita dei 131/D3

Crescenzio, Via 130/B1-132/B4

Crispi, Via Francesco 131/F2-134/A4

Cristina di Svezia, Largo 130/A6-B6

Croce, Via della 131/D1-E1

Crociferi, Via dei 131/E3

Cucchi, Piazza Francesco 136/B3

D

D'Azeglio, Via Massimo 134/C5-C6

Daini, Piazzale dei 134/B2

Dalamzia, Piazza 135/D2

Dalla Chiesa, Via Generale 132/C3

Damiata, Via 132/C3

Dandini, Via Gerolamo 138/A5-A6

Dandolo, Via 136/C3

Dante, Piazza 139/D2

Dardanelli, Via 132/B3

Dataria, Via della 134/A6

De Gasperi, Via Alcide 132/B5

De Lollis, C., Via 135/E6-F5

De Nicola, E., Viale 134/C5

De Pretis, Via Agostino 134/B6

Dogana Vecchia, Via della 130/C3

Domus Aurea, Viale 138/B2-C2

Donna Olimpia, Piazza di 136/A5

Donna Olimpia, Via di 136/A4-B6

Doria, Via Andrea 132/A4-B3

Druso, Via 138/C4

Due Macelli, Val 131/F1-F2

Duilio, Via 132/C3

Dunant, Piazzale Enrico 136/B6

E

Einaudi, Via Luigi 134/D5

Eleniana, Via 139/E2

Emo, Via Angelo 132/A4-A5

Emporio, Piazza dell' 137/D4-E4

Epiro, Piazza 139/D5

Eroi, Piazzale degli 132/A4

Esquilino, Piazza dell' 134/C6

Etruria, Via 139/D4-E5

F

Fabricio, Ponte 131/D6

Fabrizi, Viale Nicola 136/C3

Falconieri, Via Paola 136/A6-A5

Falisei, Via d. 139/E1

Farnese, Piazza 130/B5-C5

Farnese, Via Alessandro 133/D3-D4

Farnesi, Via di 130/B5

Farnesina, Lungotevere della 130/A5-B6

Faustina, Via Anna 137/F5

Febo, Largo 130/C3

Ferrari, Via Giuseppe 132/C2-C3

Ferratellani Lateramo, Via d. 138/C4

Fienili, Via dei 131/E6-F6

Filiberto, Via Emanuele 139/D2-D3

Fiorentini, Lungotevere dei 130/A3

Fioritto, Largo Enzo 138/A5

Firdusi, Piazza 133/F2

Fiume, Piazza 134/C3

Flaminia, Via 133/D1-E3

Flaminio, Piazzale 133/E3

Flamino, Lungotevere 133/D1

Florida, Via 131/D5

Fontanella Borghese, Via 131/D1

Fontanella di Borghese, Largo 131/D2

Fonteiana, Piazza 136/A4

Fonteiana, Via 136/A3-A5

Fori Impseriali, Via dei 131/F5-138/B2

Fornaci, Via delle 132/B6-136/B1

Fornaci, Via Nuova delle 136/B1-B3

Foro Piscario, Via del 131/F5

Francesco dell' Ongaro, Via 136/C4-C5

Franklin, Via Beniamino 137/D5

Frattina, Via 131/E1-E2

Frentani, Via dei 135/D5-E5

Funari, Via dei 131/D5

G

Galeno, Piazza 135/D3-E3

Galeria, Piazza 139/D6

Gallia, Via 138/C4-139/D4

Gallo, Via d. 130/B5

Galsomini, Largo Manlio 137/E4-E5

Galvani, Via 137/D5-E5

Garibaldi, Piazzale Giuseppe 136/B2

Garibaldi, Ponte 130/C6

Garibaldi, Via Giuseppe 130/A6-136/B3

Gelsomini, Viale Manlio 137/E5

Genovesi, Via dei 137/D3-E3

Germanico, Via 132/B4-C4

Gessi, Via Romolo 137/D4

Gesù, Via del 131/D4

Ghiberti, Via Lorenzo 137/D5

Gianicolense, Circonval-lazione 136/B6-C6

Gianicolense, Lungotevere 130/A5-132/C6

Gianicolo, Passeggiata del 136/B1-B2

Giardino Zoologica, Piazzale del 134/A2

Giardino Zoologico, Viale del 134/A2-B2

Gioberti, Via Vincenzo 134/C6

Giolitti, Via Giovanni 134/C6-139/E2

Giotto, Viale 138/A5

Giovagnoli, Via Raffaele 136/B4

Giovanni da Castel Bolognese, Via 136/C5-C6

Giovanni da Empoli, Via 137/E6

Giovanni, Piazza XXIII 130/A2

Giovine Italia, Piazza 132/B3

Giubbonari, Via dei 130/C5

Giulia, Via 130/A3-B5

Giuliana, Via della 132/B2-B3

Giustiniani, Piazza Orazio 137/D5

Glorioso, Viale 136/C3

Gobetti, Viale Pietro 135/D5-E5

Governo Vecchio, Via del 130/B3-B4

Gracchi, Via dei 132/B4-133/D3

Grazioli, Piazza 131/E4

Greci, Via dei 133/E4-F4

Gregoriana Via 131/F1

Gregorio VII, Via 132/A6

Guerrazzi, Via Francesco Dom. 136/B5

Guglia, Via della 131/E2

Guinizelli, Via Guido 136/B6-B5

Gustiniani, Via 130/C3-131/D3

I

Impresa, Via dell' 131/D2-E3

Independenza, Piazza dell' 134/C5-135/D5

Industria, Ponte dell' 137/D6

Innocenzo X, Via 136/A4

Innocenzo XIII, Via 132/A6-B6

Italia, Corso d' 134/C2-C3

K

Klitsche, Viale Antonietta 136/C3-C4

L

La Spezia, Via 139/E3-F3

Labicana, Via 138/B2-C2

Lancellotti, Piazza 130/B3

Lanciani, Via R. 135/F1

Lanza, Via Giovanni 138/B1-C1

Lata, Via 131/E4

Laterani, Via de 139/D3-D4

Latina, Via 139/D5-D6

Latina, Via 139/D6-F6

Lavatore, Via del 131/F2-F3

Lazzerini, Largo Carlo 138/A5

Lentari, Via del 130/C4

Leone IV, Via 132/B3-B4

Leopardi, Largo Giacomo 138/C1

Lepanto, Via 132/D2

Liberta, Piazza della 133/D3-D4

Liegi, Viale 134/B1-C1

Lorenza, Via Porto di 135/E6

Lucchesi, Via dei 131/F3

Luce, Via della 137/D2-D3

Ludovico di Monreale, Via 136/A4

Ludovisi, Via 134/A4

Luna, Via della 131/D2

Lungara, Via della 130/A6-132/C6

Lungaretta, Via della 137/D2-E2

Luzzatti, Via Luigi 139/E2

M
Maddalena, Via delle 131/D3
Madonna della Salette, Piazza 136/A6
Madonna di Loreto, Piazza 131/E4-F4
Maggio XXIV, Via 131/F3-F4
Magna Grecia, Via 139/D4-E3
Magnanapoli, Largo 131/F4-138/A1
Malpasso Vicolo 130/A3-B3
Mameli, Via Goffredo 136/C3
Manara, Via Luciano 136/C3-137/D3
Manuzio, Via Aldo 137/D5-E4
Manzoni, Viale Allessandro 139/D2-E1
Marcello, Largo Benedetto 134/C2
Marco Polo, Viale 137/F5-138/B6
Margana, Piazza 131/E5
Margana, Via 131/E5
Margherita, Ponte 133/D3-E3
Margutta, Via 133/E4-F4
Marina, Piazza della 133/E2
Marmorata, Via 137/E4-E5
Marrucini, Via d. 135/E5-E6
Marsala, Via 134/C5-135/D6
Marzio, Lungotevere 130/C1-C2
Mascherino, Via 132/B4-B5
Mascherone, Via 130/B5
Massimi, Piazza d. 130/C4
Massimo, Via Fabio 132/C3-C3
Mastai, Piazza 137/D4
Mastro Giorgio, Via 137/D4-E5
Mattei, Piazza 131/D5
Matteotti, Ponte Giacomo 133/D2-D3
Matteucci, Via Pellegrino 137/E6-F6
Mattonato, Via del 137/C2
Mazzini, Piazza Giuseppe 132/C2
Mazzini, Ponte Giuseppe 130/A4-A5
Mazzini, Viale Giuseppe 132/B2-133/D2
Mecenate, Via 138/C2
Medici, Via Giacomo 136/B3-C3
Mellini, Lungotevere 130/C1-133/D3
Mercantini, Via Luigi 136/B3
Mercede, Via della 131/E2
Merulana, Via 138/C1-139/D3
Metaponto, Via 139/D4
Metronio, Piazzale 138/C4

Metronio, Viale 138/C4-139/D5
Michelangelo, Lungotevere 133/D3
Mignanelli, Piazza 131/E1-F1
Milano, Via 134/B6
Milizie, Viale delle 132/B3-133/D3
Minerva, Piazza della 131/D4
Minghetti, Via Marco 131/E3
Monserrato, Via di 130/B4-B5
Monte Brianzo, Via 130/C2
Monte della Farina, Via del 130/C4-C5
Monte Giordano, Via di 130/B3
Monte Grappa, Piazza 133/D2
Monte Martini, Largo 132/C5
Monte Oppio, Viale del 138/B1-C1
Monte Santo, Via 132/B2-C1
Monte Savello, Piazza 131/D6-E6
Monte Testaccio, Via di 130/C4-C5
Monte Zebio, Via 132/C2-133/D1
Montecitorio, Piazza di 131/D3
Monterone, Via di 131/D4
Montevecchio, Via d. 130/B3
Monticello, Via del 131/F3
Monza, Via 139/E3
Morgagni, Via G.B.135/D4-E3
Moro, Via del 130/B6-136/D2
Morosini, Via Emilio 137/D3
Muggia, Via 132/B1-B2
Mura Aurelie, Viale delle 136/B3-B2
Mura Gianicolensi, Viale delle 136/B3-C4
Mura Latine, Via delle 138/C5-139/D6
Muratte, Via delle 131/E3
Muro Torto, Viale del 133/E3-134/A4
Museo Borghese, Viale del 134/A3-B3

N
Napoleone III, Via 134/C6-139/D1
Nari, Via d. 131/D4
Navi, Lungotevere delle 133/D2
Navicella, Via della 138/B3-C4
Navona, Piazza 130/C3-C4
Nazionale, Via 134/A6-B5

Nenni, Ponte Pietro 133/D3
Nicolò III, Via 132/B6
Nicosia, Piazza 130/C2
Nievo, Piazza Ippolito 136/C4
Nievo, Piazza Primo 136/C4
Nievo, Via Ippolito 136/C5
Nizza, Via 134/C3-135/D2
Nola, Via 139/E3
Nomentana, Via 134/C3-135/F1
Nomentana, Via 135/F1
Novembre IV, Via 131/F4
Numa Pompilio, Piazzale 138/B4
Nuovi, Via B. 130/A3-B3

O
Oberdan, Lungotevere 133/D1
Orfani, Via d. 131/D3
Orlando, Via Vittorio - Emanuele 134/B5
Oro, Piazza dell' 130/A3
Orso, Via dell' 130/C3
Orti di Cesare, Via degli 136/C6
Orvieto, Via 139/F3
Oslavia, Via 132/C1-C2
Ostiense, Piazzale 137/E5-F5
Ostiense, Via 137/E5-E6
Ottaviano, Via 132/B4
Ottavilla, Piazza 136/A4

P
Pace, Via d. 130/B3-C3
Pacinotti, Via A. 136/C6-137/D6
Paisiello,Via Giovanni 134/B1-B2
Palatino, Ponte 137/E2
Palestro, Via 134/C4-135/D5
Pallacorda, Via di 131/D2
Pallaro, Largo del 130/C5
Pallotti, Piazza Vincenzo 130/B5-B6
Panatelo, Piazza di 130/C4
Panetteria, Via della 131/F2-F3
Panico, Via di 130/A3-B3
Panisperna, Via 134/B6
Pannonia, Via 138/C4
Paoli, Piazza Pasquale 130/A3
Paolo II, Via 132/B5
Papa, achille, Via 132/C1
Paradiso, Piazza del 130/C4
Paradiso, Piazza del 130/C4
Parini, Via Giuseppe 136/C6
Parione, Via del' 130/B3-B4
Parlamento, Piazza del 131/D2
Parrasio, Via Giano 136/C5-C6
Partigiani, Piazzale dei 138/A6

Pascarella, Via Cesare 136/C5
Pasquino, Piazza di 130/C4
Pastini, Via dei 131/D3
Pellegrino, Via del 130/B4-C4
Pellicia, Via della 137/D2
Pellico, Via Silvio 132/B3-C3
Penitenza, Via della 130/A5
Penitenzieri, Via dei 132/C5-C6
Penna, Via della 133/E3-E4
Perosi, Largo Lorenzo 130/A4
Pettinari, Via dei 130/B6-C5
Pia, Piazza 130/A2
Pianellari, Via d. 130/C2
Piave, Via 134/C3-C4
Piè di Marmo, Via de 131/D4-E4
Piemonte, Via 134/B3-B4
Pierleoni, Lungotevere dei 131/E6-137/E2
Pietra, Piazza di 131/D3-E3
Pigna, Piazza d. 131/D4
Pilo, Piazza Rosolino 136/B4
Pilotta, Piazza della 131/F3
Pilotta, Via della 131/F3-F4
Pinciana, Porta 134/A3-B3
Pinerolo, Via 139/E4-F4
Pio XII, Piazza 132/C5
Pio, Borgo 132/B5-C5
Piombo, Vicolo del 131/E4
Piramide Cestia, Viale 137/E5-F5
Pisacane, Via Carlo 136/B5
Pisanelli, Via 133/E2-E3
Pisani, Via Vittor 132/A4
Piscinula, Piazza 137/E2
Pitagora, Piazza 134/B1
Plebiscito, Via del 131/F4
Po, Via 134/B3-C2
Poerio, Via Alessandro 136/B5-C4
Policlinico, Viale del 134/C4-135/F4
Pollarola, Piazza 130/C4
Pollione, Via Asinio 137/E4-E5
Polverona, Vicolo del 130/B5-C5
Pompeo Magno, Via 132/C4-133/D3
Ponte Lungo, Piazza di 139/E
Ponte S. Angelo, Piazza 130/A2
Ponte Sublico 137/D4
Ponte Testaccio, Piazzale di 136/D5-137/D6
Ponte Umberto, Piazza 130/B2-C2
Popolo, Piazza del 133/F3
Porcari, Via Stefano 132/B4-C4
Porta Angelica, Via di 132/B4-B5
Porta Ardeatina, Viale di 138/B5-C6

Porta Capena, Piazza di 138/F3-138/A3
Porta Cavalleggeri, Largo di 132/B6
Porta Labicana, Via di 139/E1-E2
Porta Latina, Via di 138/C5
Porta Lavernate, Via di 137/E4
Porta Maggiore, Piazza di 139/E2
Porta Maggiore, Via 139/D2
Porta Metronia, Piazza di 138/C4
Porta Pia, Piazzale di 137/D3-D4
Porta Portese, Piazza 137/D3-E3
Porta Princiana, Via di 134/A4
Porta Ripetta, Piazza 130/C1
Porta S. Giovanni, Piazza di 139/D3
Porta S. Lorenzo, Piazza di 139/E1
Porta S. Lorenzo, Via di 135/E6
Porta S. Pancrazio, Via di 136/C3
Porta S. Paolo, Piazza di 137/F5
Porta S. Sebastiano, Via di 138/C5-C6
Porta Tiburtina, Via di 135/D5-E6
Portico d'Ottavia, Via del 131/D5-D6
Porto Fluviale, Via del 137/D6-E6
Portuense, Lungotevere 137/D4-D5
Portuense, Via 136/C5-D4
Pozzetto, Via del 131/E2
Prati degli Strozzi, Piazza dei 132/B2
Prati, Lungotevere 130/B2-C1
Prefetti, Via dei 131/D2
Prenestina, Via 139/F2
Prestinari, Via Marcello 132/C1-133/D2
Pretoriano, Viale 135/D5-D6
Princiana, Via 134/A4
Principe Amadeo Savoia-Aosta, Ponte 132/C6
Principe Eugenio, Via 138/D1
Principe Umberto, Via 139/D1-E1
Provincie, Viale delle 135/F3-F4
Publici, Clivo dei 137/E3-F3

Q
Quattro Fontane, Via delle 134/A5-B5
Quattro Novembre, Via 134/A6-137/F1

Quattro Venti, Piazzale dei 136/B5
Quattro Venti, Viale dei 136/B3-B6
Quercia, Piazza della 130/B3-C3
Quirinale, Piazza del' 131/F3
Quirinale, Via del 134/C5
Quiriti, Piazza dei 134/A6-B5

R
Ramni, Via dei 135/E6
Re di Roma, Piazza dei 139/E4
Reggio Emilia, Via 134/C3-135/D3
Regina Elena, Viale 135/E3-F5
Regina Margherita, Piazza 135/D3
Regina Margherita, Viale 134/C1-135/D3
Regolo, Via Attilio 133/C4
Renella, Via della 137/D2
Repubblica, Piazza della 134/B5-C5
Reti, Via dei 135/F6
Revoltella, Via Pasquala 136/A6
Riari, Via dei 130/A5-136/C1
Rinascimento, Corso 130/C3-C4
Ripa Grande, Porto di 137/D4-E3
Ripa, Lungotevere 137/E3-E2
Ripetta, Via di 133/E3-E5
Risorgimento, Piazza del 132/B4
Risorgimento, Ponte del 133/D2
Rolli, Via Ettore 136/C5-C6
Romagna, Via 134/B3-B4
Romagnosi, Via -Giandomenico 133/E3
Romei, Via Romeo 132/A1-A2
Rosa, Via Ercole 138/A5
Rosolino, Piazza 136/B4
Rossetti, Via Gabriele 136/B4
Rossetti, Via Raffaele 132/A2
Rotonda, Piazza della 131/D3
Rotonda, Via della 131/D3-D4
Rovere, Piazza della 132/C6
Rubattino, Via 137/D4

S
S. Alessio, Via di 137/E4-F4
S. Ammirato, Piazza 139/F6
S. Andrea della Valle, Piazza 130/C4
S. Angelo, Borgo 132/C5
S. Angelo, Ponte 130/A2

S. Anselmo, Via di 137/E4-F4
S. Apollinare, Piazza di 130/C3
S. Balbina, Piazza di 138/A4-B4
S. Bartolomeo de Vaccinari, Via 130/C6-131/D6
S. Bernardo, Piazza di 134/B5
S. Calepodio, Via 136/A4-B5
S. Cesarini, Piazza 130/A4
S. Chiara, Piazza di 131/D4
S. Claudio, Via di 131/E2
S. Cosimato, Piazza di 136/C3-137/D3
S. Costanza, Via di 135/E1-F1
S. Croce in Gerusalemme, - Piazza di 139/D2-E2
S. Croce in Gerusalemme, Via 139/D2-E2
S. Egidio, Piazza di 136/C2
S. Eustachio, Piazza di 130/C3-131/D4
S. Francesco di Sales, Via di 130/A5-136/B1
S. Giovanni in Laterano, Piazza di 139/D3
S. Giovanni in Laterano, Via di 138/B2-139/D3
S. Giovanni, Decollato, Via di 131/F6
S. Gregorio, Via di 138/A3-B3
S. Ignazio, Piazza di 131/E3-E4
S. Lorenzo, Piazza di 131/D2
S. Lorenzo, Piazzale 135/F5
S. Marcello, Via di 131/E3
S. Marco, Via di 131/E5
S. Maria della Grazie, Piazza di 132/A4
S. Maria Liberatrice, Piazza di 137/D4
S. Maria Maggiore, Piazza di 134/C6
S. Maria Maggiore, Via di 134/B6-C6
S. Martino d. Battaglia, Via 135/D4-D5
S. Melania, Via di 137/E4
S. Michele, Via di 137/D3-E3
S. Nicola de Cesarini, Vicolo di 131/D5
S. Onofrio, Salita di 132/C6
S. P. alla Regola, Via 130/C5
S. Pancrazio, Piazza di 136/A3
S. Pancrazio, Via di 136/B3
S. Pantaleo, Piazza di 130/C4
S. Pantaleo, Via di 130/C4
S. Paolo del Brasile, Viale 134/A3
S. Paolo della Croce, Via 138/B3

S. Pietro, Piazza di 132/B5
S. Pio X, Via 132/C5
S. Prisca, Piazza 137/F4
S. Prisca, Via di 137/F4
S. Quintino, Via 139/D2-E2
S. S. Apostoli, Piazza dei 131/E4-F4
S. S. Apostoli, Via dei 131/E3-E4
S. Sabina, Via di 137/E4-F3
S. Silvestro, Piazza di 131/E2
S. Simeone, Piazza 130/B3
S. Slavatore di Lauro, Piazza di 130/B2
S. Spirito, Borgo 130/A3
S. Stefano del Cacco, Via di 131/D3-E3
S. Susanna, Largo di 134/B5
S. Teodoro, Via 131/F6-138/A2
S. Tommaso d'Aquino, Via 132/A3
S. Vincenzo, Via di 131/F3
Sabotino, Via 132/B2-C2
Sacchi, Via Gaetano 136/C3
Saffi, Via Aurelio 136/C4
Saffi, Viale Aurelio 136/C4
Salandra, Via Antonio 134/B4
Salaria, Porta 134/B4
Salaria, Via 134/C1-C3
Salerno, Piazza 135/E3
Sallustiana, Via 134/B4
Sallustio, Piazza 134/C4
Salvatore, Via d. 130/C3
Salvi, Via Nicola 138/B2
Sangallo, Lungotevere dei Tebaldi 130/A3-A6
Sannio, Via 139/D3-D4
Sanzio, R. Lungotevere 130/B6-C6
Sapienza, Largo della 130/C4
Sassia, Largo 132/C5-C6
Satrico, Via 139/D5-E5
Savelli, Vicolo, 130/B4
Savoia, Via 134/C3-D2
Savoia, Via Ferdinando di 133/E3
Savoia, Via Luisa di 133/E3
Scala, Via della 136/C2
Scalo S. Lorenzo, Viale dello 139/F1
Scanderberg, Piazza 131/F3
Scarlatti, Via Alessandro 134/B1-C2
Scauro, Clivo di 138/B3
Schiavoni, Largo degli 131/D1
Scienze, Via de 135/E5
Scimmia, Vicolo 130/A4
Scipioni, Via degli 132/B4-133/D3
Scortia, Via della 130/C1-C3
Scrofa, Via della 130/C1-C3
Scuderie Via d. 131/F2
Segneri, Via Paolo 136/C5-C6

Sella, Via Quintino 135/B4-C4
Selveri, Via D. 132/B6
Seminario, Via del 131/D3
Serpenti, Via dei 134/C6-138/B1
Servili, Piazza dei 137/E4
Settembrini, Via Luigi 132/C2-133/D3
Settembrini XX, Via 134/B5-C5
Siculi, Piazza del 135/E6
Siena, Piazza di 134/A2-A3
Siria, Via 139/E5-E6
Sistina, Via 131/F1
Sisto V, Piazzale 135/D6-E6
Sisto, Ponte 130/B6
Soana, Via 139/D4
Socrate, Piazzale 132/A3
Soldati, Via dei 130/C2
Solferino, Via 134/C5
Sora, Via 130/B4
Spagna, Piazza di 131/E1-133/F4
Specchi, Via degli 130/D5
Staderai, Via dergli 130/C3-C4
Stamperia, Via della 131/F2-F3
Statilia, Via 139/D1-E2
Statuto, Via dello 138/C1
Stazione di S. Pietro, Via della 132/B6-136/A1
Stazione Ostiense, Via della 137/E6-F6
Stelletta, Via della 130/C3-131/D2
Sublicio, Ponte 137/D4
Sudario, Via del 130/C4-131/D4

T
Taranto, Via 139/E3-F4
Tassoni, Largo 130/A3
Tata Giovanni, Via di 138/A5
Teatro di Marcello, Via del 131/E5-137/E2
Teatro Pace, Via del 130/C3-C4
Teatro Valle, Lago del 130/C4
Teatro Valle, Via del 130/C4
Tebaldi, Lungotevere dei 130/A4-B5
Tempio di Diana, Piazza del 137/E4-F4
Tempio di Giove, Via del 131/E6
Tempio, Via del 131/D6
Terenzio, Via 132/C4
Terme Deciane, Via delle 137/F3-F4
Terme di Caracalla, Largo - delle 138/B6-C6
Terme di Caracalla, Via delle 138/A4-C6
Testaccio, Ponte 137/D5
Teulada, Via 132/B1-B2

Teutro Valle, Largo del 130/C4
Thorwaldsen, Piazza 133/F2
Tiburtina, Piazzale 135/E6
Tiburtina, Via 135/E6-F5
Tiziano, Viale 133/D1-E1
Toja, Piazza Alessandro 136/C5
Tomacelli, Via 131/D1
Toniolo, Largo Giuseppe 130/C3
Tor di Nona, Lungotevere -di 130/A2-B2
Tor Millina, Via di 130/B3-C3
Tor Sang, Piazza 130/C3
Torino, Via 134/B5-C6
Torre Argentina, Largo d. 131/D4
Torre Argentina, Via di 131/D4
Traforo, Via 134/A5
Trasimeno, Piazza 135/D1-D2
Trastevere, Viale di 136/C6-137/D2
Traversari, Via Ambrogio 136/B6-C5
Trenta Aprile, Viale 136/C3
Trento, Piazza 135/D2
Trevi, Piazza di 130/F3
Triboniano, Via 130/B1-B2
Tribunali, Piazza dei 130/B2
Trieste, Corso 135/E1-D2
Trilussa, Piazza 130/B6
Trinità dei Monti, Viale della 133/F4
Trionfale, Circonvallazione 132/A2-A3
Trionfale, Largo 132/B3
Trionfale, Via 132/A1-B3
Tritone, Via del 131/E2-134/A5
Turati, Via Filippo 134/C6-139/D1
Tuscolana, Via 139/E4-F5
Tuscolo, Piazza 139/D4

U
Uffici del Vicario, Via 131/D2-D3
Ulpiano, Via 130/B1-C1
Umberto I, Ponte 130/B2-C1
Umberto I., Traforo 134/A5
Umilta, Via dell' 131/E3-F3
Ungheria, Piazza 134/B1
Unita, Piazza dell' 132/C4
Universita, Viale dell' 135/D5-E4
Urbana, Via 134/B6-138/B1

V
Vacche, Vicolo delle 130/B3
Valdina, Vicolo 131/D2
Valla, Via Lorenzo 136/B6-C6

Vallati, Lungotevere dei 130/B6-C6
Valle delle Camene, Via 138/B3-B4
Vantaggio, Via del 133/E4
Varisco, Via A. 132/A2
Vascello, Via del 136/B3-B4
Vaticano, Lungotevere 130/A5-B4
Vaticano, Viale 132/A5-B4
Venezia, Piazza 131/E4-E5
Venti Settembre, Via 134/B5-C4
Vercelli, Via 139/F4
Verdi, Piazza Giuseppe 134/D1
Vergini, Via delle 131/E3
Vespasiano, Via 132/B4
Vetrina, Vicolo della 130/B3
Villa Pamphili, Via di 136/A3-B5
Villa Peretti, Largo di 134/C5
Viminale, Piazza del 134/B6
Viminale, Via 120/B6-C5
Virgilio, Via 130/A1-132/C4
Vite, Via della 131/E1-E2
Vitelleschi, Via Giovanni 132/C5
Vitellia, Via 136/A3-A4
Vittoria, Lungotevere della 132/C1-133/D1
Vittorio Emanuele II, Ponte 130/A2-A3
Vittorio Emanuelle II, Piazza 139/D1
Vittorio Emmanuelle II, Corso 130/A3-131/D4
Vittorio Veneto, Via 134/A4-A5
Volpato, Via G. 136/C6
Volturno, Via 134/C5

Z
Zabaglia, Via Nicola 137/E5-E6
Zama, Piazza 139/E5
Zanardelli, Via 130/C2-C3
Zoccolette, Via delle 130/C6
Zucchelli, Via 130/F1-F2